SELECTED
Tips from

A BANTAM PREMIUM BOOK

BANTAM BOOKS

TORONTO · NEW YORK · LONDON · SYDNEY · AUCKLAND

OTHER BOOKS BY HELOISE

Hints from Heloise
Help! from Heloise

SELECTED TIPS FROM HELOISE
*A Bantam Book / published by arrangement with
King Features Syndicate, Inc.*

PRINTING HISTORY

Bantam Premium edition / June 1984

*Bantam Books are published by Bantam Books, Inc.
Its trademark, consisting of the words "Bantam
Books" and the portrayal of a rooster, is Registered
in U.S. Patent and Trademark Office and in other
countries. Marca Registrada. Bantam Books, Inc.,
666 Fifth Avenue, New York, New York 10103.*

PRINTED IN THE UNITED STATES OF AMERICA

CONTENTS

INTRODUCTION

Hello, everyone. I have put together some of my favorite hints for you here, and I hope that I have covered any problems you might have.

I think that you will enjoy reading through the hints, and I bet you'll find yourself saying, "Now, why didn't I think of that!" Many times, too, you may say, "I thought everyone knew that . . ." Well, that's what my column and books are all about—sharing ideas with others to make life easier for all of us.

Often these little hints are soooo simple you will kick yourself for not having thought of them. Those are the ones that I like the best . . . like putting your hand in a plastic bag and inverting it over a head of lettuce instead of trying to stuff the lettuce in the bag, or adding a cup of water to the bottom of the broiler pan before you cook anything so there is no burned-on grease, or using the spin cycle of your washing machine to damp dry your hand-washed clothes.

It seems you all have a favorite little tip, some clever shortcut you have been taking for years. If you see your tip in this book, you can say to your friends, "See, I knew I had a good idea!" And if it isn't here, why not drop me a line at P. O. Box 32000, San Antonio, Texas 78216? I will try to put your hint in my column or next book. Because of the tremendous volume of mail, I cannot respond to your questions personally, but love to hear from you.

My best to you and may all your household problems be small ones.

—Hugs, HELOISE

Chapter 1

CREATIVE CLEANING

Dear Fellow Homemakers: Cleaning chores just never seem to go away, do they? No sooner do you wash the dinner dishes, straighten the living room and hang up the coats that everyone should have hung up when they came home—then it's time to make the beds and soak the breakfast oatmeal pot. A never-ending chain of trivial but trying tasks.

How to get around them? With shrewdness and humor. It's just incredible—all the clever shortcuts you folks out there have contrived!

The work never comes to an end. But I never stop marveling at how ingenious you all are at lightening the load.

This chapter shares with you some of the best of the clever cleaning tips y'all have shared with me over the years.

FOR PEOPLE WHO HATE HOUSEWORK

The 20-minutes-a-day plan

Every day set aside exactly 20 minutes, no more, no less. Do one task you don't consider a daily or weekly chore.

Clean one drawer, wash one shelf or polish silver. Whatever you do, limit yourself to exactly 20 minutes.

In a few months you'll never have to face a major cleanup again.

The stay-put plan

Here's my secret for getting the cleaning done.

Once you start to clean a room, never leave it.

Don't go down the hall to replace mislaid things in the kitchen or the bathroom. You will get side-tracked.

Make piles at the door of the room you're working in for each of the other rooms. Baskets or trays come in handy here.

When room number one is clean, deliver the out-of-place items to the other rooms and start on the next room.

If you have an upstairs, don't go downstairs until your upstairs work is finished.

GLOVES

Bigger is better

Try using rubber gloves one size too large. They are much more convenient for kitchen use because you can slip them on and off quickly.

The larger size is easy to get used to—and the next time the phone rings while you're washing dishes, you won't have to go into a dither trying to pull off tight gloves.

Recycling rubber

Why throw away old rubber gloves? They can give you rubber bands in various sizes and colors, handy for all sorts of things.

For small rubber bands, cut across the glove fingers. For larger bands, cut across the palms and cuffs. And you can cut the bands as wide or narrow as you wish.

Help for broom handles

Another good way to use torn gloves is to cut off the rubber fingers and slip them over the handles of mops and brooms. This keeps the handles from scratching walls and the mops and brooms from falling down.

If a rubber finger does not fit a handle tightly, use a rubber band to hold the finger in place.

Glove savers

Stuff a bit of cotton into the fingertips of your rubber gloves. It will prevent your fingernails from poking holes in the rubber tips.

Wearing cotton gloves under the rubber ones will protect the tips too.

Glove trick

Right-handed? Then your right glove will usually wear out before your left. But save that left glove. When another right wears out, you'll have two lefts. Turn one inside out and you'll have a pair.

Left-handed? Then do the reverse.

Glove inside outer

To turn a rubber glove inside out, fold over the cuff and give the glove a sharp shake—you're halfway there.

Now, holding the glove over your mouth, blow into it and seal in the air with one hand. Squeeze the air toward the fingers with your other hand and the fingers will pop out.

You may need to blow twice to get all the fingers reversed.

Quick fix for gloves

Small holes or rips in rubber gloves are easy to repair. Just cut a small patch from the glove cuff, then spread a drop of rubber-bonding glue around the hole. Place the patch on the glue and hold in place with a toothpick.

Warning: if you use instant-type glue, don't touch it with your fingers. Also, don't let the glue seep through the hole into the inside of the glove or it will stick to itself.

Inside tip

Try wearing cotton gloves inside your rubber gloves

when washing dishes. It feels more comfortable, makes the rubber gloves last longer, insulates better from heat—and your hands won't perspire as much.

Hint for hands

Talcum powder eases removal of gloves and saves your hands. But don't dump the stuff into the gloves —sprinkle it on your skin. That way the powder will not cake if your hands perspire.

TOWELS

Terry roller towel

Here's a nifty way to beat the price of paper towels for drying hands in the kitchen.

Take a terry towel, fold one end over to make a pocket, then sew flat. Slip the paper tube from a used-up roll of paper towels through the pocket and replace in your paper towel roller.

You've now got a terry roller towel that can be easily washed and put back up. Make a couple.

Towel necklace

When doing any kind of cleaning job that requires paper towels, such as cleaning windows, wear the roll around you necklace-fashion.

Just run a length of cord or string through a half-used roll of paper towels (a full roll would be uncomfortably bulky), and tie it on.

Now it's always with you as you work. One less thing to carry up the ladder with you!

Reach for terry

Hang a small hand terry towel (a cup hook works fine) next to the roll of paper towels in your kitchen. Instead of using disposable towels all the time, reach for terry and make that paper roll last a little longer.

Towel chopper

From P.S.H. — I use paper towels in my kitchen and bath and in my boat galley.

To save on their use, I slice each new roll of toweling nearly in half, stopping short of the cardboard core.

I find half a towel is sufficient for quick wipe-ups. If more is needed for large spills or jobs, then just tear off both sides.

Make your own dish towels

Instead of buying expensive dish towels, buy a length of good quality terry cloth.

Cut it to dish towel size and hem it or edge it with seam binding in bright colors to complement your kitchen.

Diaper dryer

Instead of expensive decorator towels, try drying your dishes with diapers. Great if all you want is a utility-type dish towel.

You'll save a bundle and the diapers get the job done beautifully.

Towel storage

To better utilize limited kitchen drawer space, roll your dish towels and cloths after folding them and place them lengthwise in the drawer.

You'll get more items in the drawer and it will always be neat.

Color signals

This tip works if you generally color-coordinate your paper toweling and toilet tissue.

Buy a roll in a color you dislike and store it in the back of your closet. When you see that hated color you'll know it's time to lay in a new supply.

Recycle old towels

When bath towels wear thin in the middle, yet the ends are still good, cut the towel up into squares, then sew several layers of nylon net to one side of each square.

They make wonderful dishcloths.

WASHING DISHES

Fill the sink first

Do you know what you get when you put liquid dishwashing detergent in the sink while the water is running? Foam. Lots of it.

Wise up. Fill the sink with water first. Then add the detergent. That way the detergent washes your dishes and doesn't get lost in bubbles. And you're not plagued with having to waste time and water getting unwanted suds out of the sink.

Terry cushion

When washing crystal and delicate china, line the sink with a terry cloth towel. The soft fabric acts as a cushion and guards against chips and scratches.

Cushions your nerves, too!

Suds-a-scope

The next time you accidentally drop a small object into your dishwater, use a tall clear glass jar or tumbler to look through the suds to the bottom of the sink to find what you want to pick up.

Surprise. The glass magnifies.

Works in the dishwasher, too. Great for locating cutlery in the water at the bottom of the dishwasher.

Lovely lemons

Save partly used lemons and put them in your dishwater. Makes the water—and the dishes—smell nice.

If you have too many used lemons to use at one time, drop them in a plastic bag and store in the freezer.

Sterilizing dishes

Here's a dishwashing tip for homemakers without a machine.

Keep a small bottle of bleach beside your dishwashing detergent. (An old detergent bottle clearly labeled would be good.) Add a few drops of bleach to the dishwater whenever you do the dishes.

There's no danger of poisoning and you'll keep from transferring illness from one member of the family to another.

Air is best

If you do your dishes by hand, let them air dry. Much cleaner than toweling dry, unless you always use a fresh towel.

Coffee-stain remover

Here's how to get coffee stains out of plastic dinnerware.

Sprinkle a small amount of baking soda on a damp dishcloth and gently rub the stains. They should come right off and the cups won't be harmed.

For more stubborn stains, soak the cups a few seconds in a very mild solution of water and liquid chlorine bleach. (Use about one-eighth cup bleach to one quart warm water). Wash the cups and rinse them well after soaking in the bleach solution.

Never soak plastic dinnerware in a strong solution of bleach. While the stains will disappear more quickly, so will the finish on the dishes.

No-no, except sometimes . . .

Of course, we all know it's a no-no to put plastic dishes in the dishwasher as a daily routine. That caustic dishwasher detergent can eventually take off the glaze. But it's great for once-in-a-while cleaning to remove stubborn coffee and tea stains.

Get a load's worth

A hint to keep cabinets neat and clean . . .

When you do not have a full load of dishes for the dishwasher but need to do the dishes anyway, add some seldom used dishes from the cabinet shelves.

While they are washing, wipe out your cabinet shelves so they will be clean and ready to receive the clean dishes.

Your dishes will always be clean and ready to use at a moment's notice.

Rotate your crockery

Here's a hint for small households.

When taking dishes from the cupboard, take them from the top of the pile, but when returning them, put them on the bottom. That way all the dishes are kept clean.

Dish-shelf window

Many of us live in small apartments or houses and must store company dishes in the kitchen area. When an occasion for their use arises we must wash off the greasy film that has accumulated . . . then, of course, after dinner we rewash the entire mountain of dishes.

The next time you have a party and must store away your clean company dishes, tape a window of plastic wrap across the face of the shelf.

Your dishes will stay just-washed clean until guests arrive again. And you'll only have to wash them once instead of twice.

Splash stopper

For those who have a portable dishwasher or washing machine that empties into the sink with a SPLASH!—

Put a plastic or metal mesh pad (not steel wool because of rust) under the water outlet.

The pad breaks the force of the outrushing water. So there are no more spatters on the floor. Less noise, too.

Dish drainer wedge

To drain hand-washed dishes quickly and keep the rubber draining tray clean, prop the tray at a slant.

A rubber doorstop wedge or an object such as a spatula can be slid under the tray at the far end so the water will run off quickly.

It's standing water that causes the ugly lime build-up on the draining tray.

CLEANING POTS AND PANS

Bottle-cap scourer

A plastic bottle cap makes a great little scouring pad.

Use the flat open end to scrape stuck or burned-on food from pots and pans. Just wet the pan and scour away. The plastic won't scratch non-stick coating, and it's easy on your manicure.

Double scrub

Why not slice your steel-wool scouring pads in half with scissors? That way you'll never have a pad rusting before you've used up the soap.

What's more, you'll be sharpening your kitchen shears.

Plastic-bag scrubber

Instead of a cloth or sponge, use a plastic bag to scrub pots and pans with a cleanser.

You don't waste cleanser because the plastic doesn't soak it up the way a sponge does.

Grease bake-off (1)

A good way to remove burned-on grease from glass baking dishes is to use powdered copper cleanser.

Make a paste, apply to a square of nylon net or a damp paper towel and rub until the baked-on residue is gone.

Grease bake-off (2)

When all else fails, and you just can't get those

burned-on brown grease spots off your glass and whiteware oven dishes, try this.

Warm the dish in the oven, then spray the dish liberally with oven cleaner. Let it soak for a few minutes, then wash in warm sudsy water.

You may need to use a steel wool soap pad or other type scrubber to remove really stubborn spots and you may even need to repeat the whole process. But at least you'll have nice shiny dishes again.

Stove cleanup

Tired of scratching away at blackened burner catch-pans from your stove?

Simply soak them overnight in a solution of water and dishwasher detergent. In the morning go over them with a wad of nylon net.

Most of the baked-on accumulation will have slipped off and the rest vanishes with a small amount of scrubbing.

Voilà! The pans are shining again. (But wear gloves—dishwasher detergent is strong stuff.)

Casserole de-gunker

Have you ever baked a casserole and afterwards had gunk stuck on the dish so badly you thought you'd have to dynamite it off?

Well, just sprinkle a little dishwasher detergent in the dish, then add hot water. Let it soak for a few hours, overnight if it's really bad, then the only thing you have to do is lightly scrub—swish, swash—and the gunk is gone.

Cold water cure

Some people do not seem to know that cold water is

much better than hot for soaking dishes and pans that have dried egg or milk on them.

The hot water seems to cook the food on and makes it harder to get the gook off.

Dry scrub method

Another way to remove dried-up egg from a frying pan is to scrub it out with a tissue.

Leave the emptied pan on the turned-off burner and the remaining heat will dry the egg into an easy-to-scrape-out crust.

Broiler saver

From H.W.— For years I wasted money lining my broiler with aluminum foil whenever I broiled steaks and chops. Then I found the free way to avoid scrubbing out burned-on broiler grease.

Just pour a cup of water into the pan before broiling. Grease dripping from the meat on the rack dissolves in the water, and any residue washes right out.

SPILLS AND BROKEN GLASS

Quick spill picker-upper

When something spills onto your carpet, grab a spoon or your pancake turner and a bowl.

Lift up the mess into the bowl and keep scraping the carpet until it is almost dry.

Wipe up the remainder with a damp towel; then, if need be, go over the spot with a little white vinegar and water to keep the carpet from staining. Then pat dry.

This method has saved many a carpet cleaning bill.

Bread "broom"

From R.M.— I dropped a glass in the kitchen and it shattered into a thousand pieces. I did not have my shoes on at the time and the nearest thing I could reach was the bread.

So I used a slice to sweep up all the tiny shreds of glass. It worked well, and I didn't cut my feet.

Glass trick (1)

When shattered glass falls onto carpeting, try the old lint trick for removing it.

Make a ball of crumpled masking tape and use it to lift the glass shards out of the carpet.

Glass trick (2)

To sweep up broken glass, place a damp paper towel over the debris first.

The tiny shattered pieces will cling to the paper and all can be easily swept up.

Works with pet hair, too.

Crystal saver

From W.J.Z.— When you accidentally chip the rim of one of your precious, impossible-to-replace crystal goblets, don't sink into a fit of depression.

Instead, head for your manicure box and a plain, ordinary emery board. The short three-inch ones are easiest to work with.

Start with the fine side and, slowly and carefully, smooth off all the sharp edges, inside and out, testing with a forefinger as you work.

Then with the coarse side of the emery board, still working with care, soften and taper down the sharp corners of the chip until it becomes only a slight dip in the rim.

Finish with a little more stroking with the fine side to round the edge slightly and your precious piece of crystal is ready for service again for any guest, and not to be "reserved for myself" for fear of a cut lip!

KITCHEN BRIGHTENERS

Shining fridge

If you like gleaming appliances, wax your refrigerator with car wax. The results will delight you.

Smudges and fingerprints will just slip right off with a dry cloth. Your fridge will sparkle and so will you.

Kitchen grease cutter

Built-up grease and dust in kitchen corners and out-of-the-way places often will yield to a little rubbing alcohol. Kills germs, too.

Grape-juice stain remover

Grape juice just seems to sink right into porcelain drainboards and laminated plastic countertops. You can get those annoying purple stains out with a little silver cream applied to a damp cloth. Rub gently.

Garbage "pail"

From F.K.— I came up with a terrific solution to the problem of an accessible under-the-sink garbage container.

I purchased an oblong dishpan with cut-out handles. It holds a large-sized grocery bag perfectly. No squashing to make it fit. It's deep enough to support the bag but shallow enough so that I can get my hands in under the sink.

Once a week I use the same dishpan to hold the water when I scrub the kitchen floor. The mop fits easily into the pan and the handles make it easy to move around.

And once a week my garbage "pail" is washed!

Newsprint polish

To polish glass and chrome to a sparkling finish, just wipe off smudges with an appropriate glass cleaner or plain damp cloth.

Polish with a dry newspaper. The printer's ink makes the glass and chrome shine like never before.

ASHTRAYS

Ashtray trick

Ashtrays smell so yukky, nobody likes to clean them. To make cleaning easier, wax your clean ashtrays or spray them with vegetable oil.

Ashes won't cling, odors won't linger and tissues or paper towels (you can use soiled ones) will wipe the ashtrays clean.

Pot-pie ashtrays

For a big bash, when you never have enough ashtrays, save aluminum pot-pie tins.

They don't break or catch fire and you can just drop them into the trash after emptying.

Safety measure

After having guests, when there may be many full

ashtrays, empty them into a piece of aluminum foil (preferably used, of course) and crush tightly.

Much cleaner and safer than dumping the contents directly into the trash. Don't ever do that.

Softener sheets to the rescue

Here's a useful tip for anyone who detests cleaning out dirty ashtrays.

Save old fabric softener sheets in an empty coffee can. Then when it's time to clean the ashtrays, a sweep with the softener sheet makes them sparkle and hides the odor between washings.

Use another empty coffee can to discard all cigarette butts, cover it securely, and discard the can when full. Sure keeps the stale tobacco odor down.

Home Sweet Home

Want to make your home a more pleasant-smelling abode and mask stale smoking odors?

Try tucking a fabric softener sheet inside the vent that delivers air to a room, or tape one to a radiator.

As the fan comes on, the pleasant aroma permeates the area, and after the fan goes off the fresh smell remains for quite some time.

DUSTING AND VACUUMING

Fluffy softener mop

Here's another use for fabric softener sheets after they've served in the dryer. Make a dust mop.

Attach a little eye-screw to one end of an old

broom handle or bowl-brush handle or length of dowel rod.

Gather about a dozen used softener sheets in the middle and tie them with a string. Tie the string to the eye of the screw and spread out the sheets.

You now have a fluffy, antistatic dust mop that's good for wiping cobwebs off the ceiling or getting at hard-to-reach corners.

When the sheets get dirty, just throw them away and make a fresh mop.

Vacuum sweetener

Hate the stale smell of the vacuum cleaner?

Place half a scented fabric softener sheet inside your vacuum canister or at the bottom of the upright bag container.

Some difference when you turn on the machine. Sweet scent instead of stale!

Filling the vacuum

A new toilet bowl brush (reserved just for this purpose) can reach all the edges and hard-to-get-at corners of wall-to-wall carpeting that your upright vacuum cleaner misses.

What's more, you don't have to get down on your knees to reach the tough spots.

Cat hair cure

From F.P. — I own a volatile white Persian cat, who sheds over rugs and upholstery. My vacuum cleaner just can't cope with the hair everywhere.

Imagine my surprise to discover that an inexpensive sponge mop, dampened slightly, lifts not only sheets of cat hair, but also surface dust and sewing lint, right off the rugs.

I use the mop like a rake, pulling it in one direction. No vacuum can compare.

Help at hand

Here's a way to save all that hassle and hunting around for supplies when you are using cleaning and polishing aids.

Just use a rubber band to fasten to each bottle, jar or can its appropriate applicator—flat sponge or terry cloth to the powdered cleanser, soft flannel to the furniture wax and silver cleaner, an old piece of sheet to the window cleaner, etc.

There they are, always ready to go when you are.

Versatile oven mitts

You'd be amazed at how many uses there are for those big terry cloth oven mitts.

Great for wiping splatters off kitchen walls, the terry cloth loops scrub right into the depressions in textured paint. They also scrub vinyl floors in a flash —a huge area wipes clean in one swipe. In addition, the mitts slurp up spills, do dusting, and, if slightly dampened, pick up pet hairs from upholstery.

When finished, throw the mitts into the washer— they come out clean and ready for the next task.

TIDY TOILETS

Stubborn commode stains?

Pour in one cup of vinegar—nothing else—and let it stand overnight. After that, a few strokes of the brush and most stains should be gone. If necessary, repeat the procedure.

How to empty a toilet bowl—almost

Did you know that a bucket of water (not hot—it might split the bowl) poured quickly into the commode will carry out most of the standing water?

Great if you need to work on tough stains, and you use less cleanser too.

The ultimate bowl-brush holder

It's a flower pot! Pretty and practical. You can pick a color to match your bathroom decor, even apply decals to the pot.

Best of all, water drips through the drain holes of the pot and is caught in the saucer. No mess.

Save that bowl

Want to save your commode from getting all scratched and having to replace it or apologize every time someone uses it?

If you see scratches or what look like thin silver streaks in your toilet bowl, the culprit might be your bowl brush.

Take a look at your brush and chances are the bristles are worn down or so flattened out that the metal of the brush is scraping against the surface.

It's well worth the cost of a new brush to keep from damaging your bowl 'cause, believe you me, you will faint when you find out how much it would cost to replace it.

Take heed and go have a look!

Net helper for bowl brush

The net bags that onions and potatoes come in are

great to tie over your toilet brush. The net does a
good cleaning job, doesn't hurt the bowl, and keeps
the brush from wearing out so fast.

Drip-free bowl cleaning

Here's what to do with a wet toilet brush.

Suspend the brush over the middle of the bowl
and close the seat over the handle. Voilà. No water
on the floor.

A neater bowl-brush holder

Here's a simple solution to the problem of the dripping bowl brush. Just put a sponge at the bottom of
the brush holder. It will soak up moisture and keep
the holder neat.

A comfortable lid cover

Instead of putting the terry cloth seat-lid cover on
the back (that is, the top) of the toilet lid, put it on
the front. The colorful terry can always be seen. And
it sure is warm in winter!

PAPER TRICKS

Half a roll is better . . .

Don't wait till the toilet paper is all gone to change
the roll. Install a new roll when the old still has half a
roll or so to go. Store in the back of your linen closet.

You'll never be caught short.

A lid in time saves the bowl

If your toilet-paper holder is one of those metal ones
with a little spring inside, here's a hint that may save
you a plumber's bill:

Always put the lid down before changing the paper roll. That little spring might just pop out and slither down the hole of an open bowl.

Don't say it can't happen . . . it has, many times.

Toilet tissue money-saver

Before you install a fresh roll of paper, flatten it. Just stand right on it. Then install.

The squashed roll will go blup-blup-blup instead of r-r-r-r-r! Great when there are little hands in the house.

Paper roll basket

Can't decide whether the toilet tissue should roll from the top or the bottom of the roll? Here's a compromise.

Stand the roll in a small wicker basket hung on the bathroom wall beside your commode. The handle of the basket can be suspended on cup hooks or over curtain-rod holders.

The basket looks cute and it beats hassling with a spring roller.

BEAT THE BATHTUB BLUES

De-appliqué the bathtub . . .

When your rubber tub appliqués start looking shabby and need to be replaced, you can unglue them with plain ol' nail polish remover.

But a word of caution: use it only on porcelain tubs. Nail polish remover will damage fiberglass tubs.

. . . then unglue the glue . . .

Amazing how many people write to complain of glue residues from bathtub decals. If nail polish remover doesn't remove the glue, oil-based pre-wash spray will.

Just spray over the residue and let set a few minutes. Then apply elbow grease.

Two applications may be necessary, but the glue should roll up and come off.

. . . and get rid of stains

Sometimes, even after all the glue has been stripped from a tub, stains from decals remain. One solution is to use dishwasher detergent.

Run hot water to cover the stained area and then dissolve three tablespoons of detergent. Let stand until the stain fades.

Baking soda to the rescue

Fiberglass bathtubs and shower stalls can be difficult to keep clean, especially in hard water areas.

Here's how to get off stubborn soil. Make a paste of baking soda and leave it on the tub or stall overnight. Next day turn the water on full blast.

Most of the film should lift. Treat difficult areas by sprinkling with fresh baking soda and scrubbing with a damp cloth (not a sponge) just as you would with scouring powder.

Your fiberglass tub will gleam again.

Brush the bath

Stymied by a stubborn bathtub ring? Try using a toilet bowl brush.

No more crouching and stooping to wash the tub. And a real time-saver.

Be sure to use a separate brush for the toilet, though.

Getting rid of mildew

The best way to get rid of bathroom mildew is to nip it in the bud.

Get into the habit of taking the time (all of 60 seconds) to wipe the water residue from tiles and rims of tubs after showering or taking a tub bath, and you'll never have to cope with the black horror again.

If mildew already mars your tiles, do this:

First wash the tiles and grout with a detergent and a scrub brush. Then apply a solution of three table-spoons liquid chlorine laundry bleach to a quart of warm water.

If possible, keep surfaces wet with this solution for five minutes. Rinse and dry.

SINK SAVVY

Drainpipe refreshers

Even the best-kept kitchen sinks can get clogged once in a while. To keep your kitchen sink humming, give the drainpipe an occasional cleaning.

Pour one cup of baking soda and then one cup of vinegar into the drain. When the stuff foams up, pour in a pint of boiling water.

Or try using laundry detergent. Pour in a cupful, then follow with a half gallon of boiling water. Then flush with hot tap water.

Either method sure beats using those caustic drain cleaners!

Substitute strainer

Do scraps of food and small objects often slip down your kitchen sink because the drain's strainer holes are too large?

You can make a finer-holed strainer out of the perforated lid of an empty scouring powder can. Just cut away the paper container, then twist a small loop of wire through two holes of the lid. (A bread wrapper twistie works perfectly.)

You'll find that the lid fits right into most kitchen sink drains and lifts out easily by the twistie handle.

Stopgap stopper

From D.G.— While filling a hot water bottle one day, I dropped the bottle stopper and it fell upright into the bathroom sink drain. The sink began filling with water because the stopper fit perfectly!

So if the rubber stopper to your bathroom sink has a way of disappearing when you need it most, remember, in a pinch you can always use the top of your hot water bottle.

Chapter 2

SPRUCING UP YOUR HOME

If cleaning things were all we homemakers had to do, life would be relatively easy. Fact is—and I don't need to tell you—it's a constant battle to keep up with overflowing closets and cluttered drawers, peeling paint and loose screws.

Nobody can keep everything in apple-pie order all the time—except maybe some lucky souls who have nothing else to do. The rest of us have to fit all those maintenance and repair chores into busy days.

So do what you can. Take heart and help from the tips here, and if you have to leave tasks for to-morrow—well, take consolation in knowing you're not alone.

*—*HELOISE

STORAGE

Chain hang

Need more closet space?

Buy eighteen inches of quarter-inch brass chain.

Put one sturdy hanger through the second or third link and hang from the rod. Let the remainder of the chain dangle and put other hangers through the links as desired.

This is an excellent way to hang blouses, skirts and small-children's clothes.

You can also hang a chain in a soft garment bag. The hangers will not slip out of the links, and you get to use that wasted space at the bottom.

Or just suspend a chain from the ceiling of your closet. No telling what you can hang on it!

Vertical expansion

Double the hanging space in closets by making a second tier.

Attach two lengths of chain (heavy plastic chain works fine) to the regular rod. Slide a large-size wooden dowel rod through the links at the level you want. Let it protrude four to five inches on each side and it will stay in place.

For triple space, just add another dowel.

An old smoothie

Next time you clean a clothes closet, take a few extra seconds to rub a bit of wax over the rod. Hangers will slide along easily.

Floor wax, furniture wax, even beeswax will do it.

Cure for an ornery clothes rod

If waxing doesn't help an old metal or wooden rod, try this inexpensive solution.

Sheathe the rod with a plastic cover for a shower-curtain rod. Just cut to fit and slip over the top of the closet rod.

Hangers will glide smoothly. What a pleasure.

Organize your clothes

Help yourself and everyone in your house keep clothes arranged by making separators for the closet rods like the ones you see in clothing stores.

Use plastic lids from margarine tubs or coffee cans. Cut a slit to the center of the lid, then cut out a circle so the lid will slip over the rod. Label the lids to suit your needs: summer-winter, work-play, blouses-skirts, etc.

A great organizer, and especially helpful when a closet must be shared.

Help in the dark

Tired of fumbling in the dark for the closet-light pull chain? Just clamp on a fluorescent fish bobber.

No more fumbling. No more stumbling.

Clips in the closet

Have an under-the-stairs closet? That slanted wall (or is it a ceiling?) can give storage service. You can attach clip-type clothespins to the wall with glue.

A great way to stay jumble-free and keep gloves, scarves, caps and what-have-you right in view.

Space-saving closet door

In a small bedroom where space is at a premium, remove the closet door, and put up a window shade matching the one on your window. This allows more room because you don't have to swing open a door.

The shade hardware should be fastened to the outer edge of the closet frame, so the shade will cover the open space and provide maximum protection from dust.

The removed door can be laid flat in your storage area or under your bed.

Homemade closet fresheners

Create your own closet fresheners inexpensively. Saturate cotton balls with oil of wintergreen or your favorite cologne. Place in a small jar, such as a pimiento jar, and punch holes in the lid.

As a precaution, keep out of reach of small children and pets.

Preventive medicine for closets

This is not the "sweetest" subject, but here's how to keep your closets from going sour.

If a garment is clean enough to wear again, don't take it off and immediately hang it in the closet.

Put the garment on a hanger and hang it on a curtain rod or over a door. Leave it out at least overnight to allow it to air.

Don't take off a damp garment and put it right back in your closet, and squash it between other clothes. The odors cannot possibly escape. Nor can the moisture it has picked up from the air . . . or from you. That's what causes closets to smell!

Hang the garment wrong side out and then hang it up to air. (Remember, you did not perspire on the outside of the garment.)

Some people say horses sweat, men perspire, and ladies "glow." But sometimes doing housework, we work like horses . . . so give your clothes the air!

Make your own cedar closet

Here's the next best thing to real cedar closets.

Get some cedar shavings at a lumber store specializing in hardwoods and make cedar sachets by filling old nylon stockings. Tie the open ends with pretty ribbon. Hang in all your closets.

Makes them smell great!

How to discourage moths

An easy way to help moth-proof out-of-season clothes is to fill an old sock or nylon stocking with moth crystals, then attach it with a rubber band over the nozzle of your electric hair dryer.

Put the dryer on a closet shelf, turn it on to *cold*—never hot, close the door and let the dryer run for ten minutes or so.

To help moth-proof clothes in a garment bag, slip the hanging ring of the dryer over a clothes hanger inside the bag.

How to strip old shelving

Everybody sure loves adhesive contact paper. There are so many things you can decorate with it. But ever try to get it off shelving? Worse than wallpaper.

Unless you try a little heat.

One way to warm up the paper so you can remove it is to use a hot iron. Protect the iron by placing old rags or paper towels over the shelf.

Then iron away. The adhesive will soften and the paper will pull off in a jiffy.

Or try a small hand hair dryer. Put it on hot and blow the heat onto the paper. As the adhesive softens, pull the paper away. This method takes a bit more time and effort, but it works.

BEDS AND SPREADS

Weight trick

From B.B.— I have a small bedroom and my bed is up against the wall. It's hard to crawl across the bed to stuff the bedspread down the far side.

My spread is a lightweight cotton, so I pinned weights—nuts and bolts—to the underside of the edge of the spread. Now it slides right down into place.

Pin trick

Some large patterned spreads are really hard to center at a glance—especially on large-sized beds.

To avoid ten trips around the bed to get the spread in place, mark the center of the spread with safety pins on the underside of the top and bottom hems.

Now when you lay the spread you have only to center the top pin between the pillows. Center the bottom pin by eye.

Quick frills

Here's a nice idea for an instant little girl's room bedspread when a child comes to visit.

Spread an old lace tablecloth over a colored sheet —pastel or bright. So pretty. Your visitor will be delighted.

Pillow bed

Short of sleeping space for overnight guests? Here's the perfect solution.

If you have a sofa with six cushions, just lay them in two rows of three on a twin-sized contour sheet on the floor. Bring the sheet up tight around the cushions.

Now lay another fitted sheet over the top. The two sheets keep the cushions together.

Makes a most comfortable bed. Good for the back, too.

Wicker-look headboard

From D.M.— I always wanted a wicker headboard but the price was beyond my budget.

So I went to the rug section of a large department store and bought two lovely woven straw mats. I hung them on the wall at the head of the bed with a few small nails.

Voilà. The wicker look I've always wanted for a fraction of the cost of a headboard!

Cord concealer

On a Hollywood bed, the electric blanket cord is inclined to protrude from under the foot of the bed. And some of us are apt to catch an ankle in it when making up the bed.

A simple remedy is to attach a cup hook to the underside of the box spring with the open part of the hook pointing toward the head of the bed.

Thread the cord through the hook and the cord will stay safely hidden.

Recycled blanket

When an electric blanket refuses to function any longer; why not rip out all the wiring and threads holding the wiring in place and have an extra blanket?

The wires can be easily stripped out by cutting tiny slits at the ends of the wires at the head and foot of the blanket. Just grab hold and pull them out. (On some blankets it may be necessary to remove the binding first.)

You'll end up with a blanket that can be easily laundered and will be useful for many more years.

CURTAINS

Easy rod insertion

Some curtain rods have such rough or sharp edges at each end that inserting them into your sheer curtains means risking damages and rips.

The cure is simple. Slip an empty chewing gum package over the rough end of the curtain rod. Mold the package to fit with your hand and the rod should go through the curtain without tearing it. Once the curtain is threaded on the rod, remove the package.

Another way to get the same result is to slip a finger from an old tissue-thin plastic glove over the rod end.

Avoiding ups and downs

When hanging curtains most folks hop on and off a stepstool to even the gathers.

Much more sensible to keep your feet on the floor and grip a yardstick, reaching up with it to adjust those gathers.

Less energy required, no teetering precariously, and you'll do a better job.

Curtain raiser

From J.C.— My kitchen windows have cafe curtains. Each time I raised the window to let in some air, the curtains would blow or get sucked into the screen and get dirty.

I got an idea and attached the curtain rod to the window itself. Now when the window is raised, the curtain goes up too.

Medicine for sick curtains

This household hint has become a standby for generations.

To give limp old curtains a refreshing lift, simply rinse them in water in which a cup of Epsom salts has been dissolved.

Makes decrepit curtains look fresh as spring.

Kitchen curtain guard

To protect curtains on a window over a sink, tuck the bottoms into a plastic bag and secure with a clip-type clothespin.

After finishing splashy, messy work, just slip off the bag and rinse it, and it's ready to be used again.

The method is useful in bathrooms, too.

A clever switch

From F.K.— My daughter wanted a change of curtains on her windows. At the time she had sheer ruffled tie-backs with draperies on each side.

So she just turned the curtains around, which placed the ruffles at the sides of the windows instead of in the center, and let the curtains hang straight rather than tied back.

Presto! Same curtains, but new look. That's my girl!

Ironing without an iron

It's a problem to press newly washed sheer panels that are too wide for the ironing board.

After washing and rinsing them, try hanging them up on their rods while still damp (but not dripping). Then line the bottom hem with fishing sinkers. The more you load into the hem, the better they pull the panels to drape just right.

Your sheers will look beautifully crisp though you never touched an iron to them.

RUGS AND CARPETING

The meaning of broadloom

Folks often ask what "broadloom" means—a type of carpet weave, a trade name, or what?

Well, at one time, the machines used for weaving carpet were 27 or 36 inches wide. These narrow pieces were sewn together to make wider pieces of carpet. Then wider machines were developed to produce carpet and these machines were called "BROADloom."

The word has now come to mean a carpet six feet or wider. It has nothing to do with the quality; it just tells you it is a wide piece of carpet.

Rescuing Scorched Carpet

Someone's dropped a cigarette and burned an inch-long hole right in the middle of your rug or carpet. Don't despair!

With curved nail scissors, cut out the blackened fibers, leaving a little pit. Cut fresh fibers from a remnant of the carpet (if you have one) or from an inconspicuous spot—under furniture, say.

Then squeeze a bit of liquid glue into the pit. Stand the replacement fibers right up in the glue. After drying, the patch will withstand wear and vacuuming—and it's practically invisible!

Why be shocked?

From J.D.— We put wall-to-wall carpeting all over our house and it seemed no matter what kind of shoes or slippers we were wearing, there was always static electricity.

It was really annoying, getting a little shock every time you touched something metal. Then I thought of antistatic laundry spray.

I gave the soles of all our slippers a good "zap," and now the sparks have stopped flying.

Curing crushed carpet

Rearranging furniture can leave stubborn indentation marks in your carpet.

One way to remedy those pesky pits is to sit an ice cube on each one. Let the ice melt and soak down overnight, then blot up any remaining moisture. The indentations should be gone.

Or you can hold your steam iron about an inch over the indentation (never touch the carpeting with the iron—it could damage the pile). Let steam pen-

etrate until it moistens the fibers and allows them to
spring back to shape.

Either way, you may need to use your hand or a
brush to fluff up the spots.

For smaller rooms

From B.P.— Commercial carpet fresheners (sold as
"rug and room deodorizers") may work well in large
open rooms. But in very close, small apartments like
mine they leave a lingering too-pungent odor.

Freshening the rug with baking soda just left the
room with a case of blahs. So I mixed the two—
carpet freshener and baking soda—in equal propor-
tions, sprinkled the mixture over the carpet, then
vacuumed.

Result: a mild, clean fragrance in my small
apartment.

Cover-up

From L.D.— I thought my bright orange bathroom
rug was ruined when I spilled bleach on it. The
white spots left by the bleach stood out like sore
thumbs.

Then I got a flash, bought a big orange felt-tipped
marker and touched up the spots. Now each time I
launder the rug I treat the spots again. Unless you
get down on your hands and knees, you don't even
see the bleach marks.

REPAIRS

Extra equipment

Keep an ear syringe, a potato peeler, some cotton-tipped swabs and a few clothespins in your tool box.

The syringe squirts oil just where you want it and picks up liquids in hard-to-reach spots. The potato peeler neatly planes wooden edges. The swabs clean motor crevices. The clothespins come in handy as lightweight clamps.

Rust preventive

Tools so often get rusty—but not if you keep some moth balls (crystals work, too) in your tool box or drawer. The stuff soaks up moisture and humidity, so your tools just don't rust.

Rust antidote

So you stored tools without oiling them? And when next you needed them, they were badly rusted or soiled?

Metal cleaners may not work, but don't lose heart. Rub the metal with shortening, then wash it off with strong soap. The tools will come out clean enough to be used again.

Handy pegboard fixture

A small roll of quarter-inch elastic can work wonders for the pegboard you hang tools on. Knot one end of the roll, and starting from the back of the board, weave the elastic through the holes as desired. Now you have loops to hold your tools.

If a tool is extra heavy, you may have to use two strands of elastic.

Good for a sewing room, too.

Reaching inconvenient oil holes

Some motors are hard to get at when oiling time comes, like the fan motor on an outside air conditioner.

You can solve the problem without removing the cover. Straighten a wire coat hanger, touch one end to the oil hole, raise the other end and drip oil onto the wire.

It flows down nicely and works every time.

Turn of the screw

If you don't have a Phillips screwdriver at hand when you need it, substitute a potato peeler.

It fits right into the crossed grooves on the screw head, so you can turn the screw easily.

Lighting the way

If you have to fix something in a dark place, tape a pencil flashlight to the tool.

This delivers plenty of light to just the right spot.

First aid for scissors

When the screw loosens in a pair of scissors, wind it in some sewing thread and set it back in place.

The thread makes the screw fit a bit tighter and should help keep the scissors together longer.

Water-resistant lubricant

Rubbing soap on the threads is a good way to help a screw penetrate wood, but not where moisture is present. Corrosion may result.

Instead, use a small cake of beeswax, available at hardware stores and notions counters. Dampness does not affect it, and it's also good for lubricating wooden drawers in chests, cabinets and desks.

Maneuvering a small screw

Sometimes fingers cannot put a tiny screw back

where it belongs. In such a case, stick the end of the screwdriver into a little glue, and the screw will adhere to it.

The screw can then be threaded back into its hole without a lot of fumbling.

Left or right?

If you are not handy, but have to work with a screwdriver or wrench and are not sure which way to turn it, remember this rhyme:

"Left loose, right tight."

The same goes for hose nozzles, the twisties securing bread wrappers, jar tops—countless other things.

First aid for loose screws

From C.R.— The lid to our piano bench kept falling off. I couldn't seem to get it fixed. Problem was that the screws were too loose in the wood.

So I took big wooden kitchen matches and put them in the holes where the screws had been. Then I broke off the matches even with the lid surface, then placed the screws back in the holes.

Result: the screws were in tight, as good as new. My piano bench was repaired.

Bigger can be better

If you can't get a loose screw to hold by stuffing a match, wood filler, steel wool or something else into the hole, don't give up.

Try driving in a screw that's one size larger. That should do the trick.

Shellac new screws

Suppose you are driving new screws into new holes. The screws will anchor better if you dip them in thinned shellac just before using them.

And you get a bonus. Shellac keeps the screws from rusting.

Storing small objects

To store various-sized screws, nails, pins and other small items, sort them into glass jars. Then nail the screw-on tops of the jars to the bottoms of eye-level shelves or other handy surfaces such as exposed workroom beams.

Screwing the jars into the lids provides safe, visible storage for all kinds of items—including those odds and ends cluttering up your drawers.

Now you'll be able to find them when you want them.

PAINTING

To keep roller fresh

If you are roller-painting a room and do not finish the same day, you can avoid the hassle of washing out the roller.

Just shove it into a plastic bag and close the bag tightly with a twistie. Next day the roller will be soft and moist, ready to go.

Less mess

Line your roller pan with heavy-duty aluminum foil. When finished with painting, just throw away the foil—and you have no messy pan to clean.

The foil lining also prevents picking up rust marks from an old pan.

Protecting windowpanes (1)

To paint around windows, cut newspaper into strips about three inches wide. Dip them in water and press them on the glass close to the wood frame.

When the painted frames are dry, moisten the newspaper with a damp sponge. The paper will peel right off, leaving the glass untouched by paint.

Protecting windowpanes (2)

An alternate way to keep panes or screens free of paint is to use the straight edge of an old dustpan. With the handle down, press the dustpan edge to the frame edge and paint away.

Saves having to tape or scrape the glass, prevents clogging the screens.

To paint screens quickly

Here's an easy way to paint screens. Run a length of cord through the hooks on top of each screen, then tie both ends of the cord to your clothesline.

Now you can paint the second side of the screen without waiting for the first side to dry.

Substitute brush for screens

To do screens without getting half the paint on everything else, forget brushes and spray cans. Paint with a small piece of tightly woven carpet tacked to a piece of flat wood.

Use the carpet as you would a brush. Dip it into the paint, rub the excess off on the inside of the paint can, and paint one side of the screen.

Let that side dry, then paint the other side. Works perfectly—no fuss, no muss.

Dating the job

When you paint a room, write the date in pencil under the switchplate—also the brand of paint and color used.

Then later if you need to know, you can always check back to see how long it has been since the room was painted and how well the particular brand held up.

Telltale marbles

Drop a couple of marbles into leftover paint before sealing and storing the can.

The marbles will become stuck in the thickened paint at the bottom of the can. When you want to use the paint again and mix it by shaking the can, you will know the paint is well mixed when you hear the marbles rattle freely.

Eyeglass wisdom

Save old eyeglasses to wear while painting inside your house, especially when you are working on ceilings or high on walls.

Paint spatters will smear and spot the old glasses rather than your nice new ones.

Handy paint container

For small paint jobs, take a clean coffee can and cut the plastic lid into a half-moon shape, leaving the lip intact so the lid still fits the can snugly.

Pour the paint into the coffee can, and use the

half-moon edge to scrape excess paint from the brush. Keeps things neat.

To save leftover paint, just snap on a whole plastic lid from another can.

Inexpensive protection

When using spray paint for small items, put each hand in a small plastic bag.

That way, you keep your hands clean without spoiling a pair of gloves.

Stockings for straining

Nylon hose can be used to strain any number of things, such as the scum that forms when leftover paint is stored.

Paint storage

Store paint cans upside down. The heavy pigment will be on top when the cans are opened, making mixing faster and easier.

Once a can is opened, make sure the lid is replaced tightly and securely before turning the can upside down. Rapping the lid rim with a hammer (over newspaper to prevent spattering) will help.

Sensible precaution

Before painting interior walls or woodwork, rub petroleum jelly on hardware that cannot be easily removed.

Paint splatters and spatters can be wiped right off the metal.

How to protect hair

If you are as messy as most amateur painters, you're sure to get paint in your hair during a job.

Unless you wear a shower cap, that is. It will catch the smears and splashes.

Slowing down plaster

When mixing plaster for patching, you may want to keep it from hardening too fast by adding cream of tartar.

But plain vinegar will work as well. Simply mix the plaster with half vinegar and half water—instead of just water.

SHORTCUTS

Scratch prevention

Jugs, vases, ceramic ashtrays, pottery pitchers, flower pots—all may have rough, scratchy bottoms, right?

Buy some rubber washers at the hardware store (if you haven't already got some cluttering up a drawer). With household glue, stick three washers in a triangle arrangement to each rough bottom.

Now your countertops, tables and shelves are safe from marring.

Easing the way

Before moving heavy appliances like a refrigerator or stove, rub the floor covering with a bar of soap or some liquid detergent.

The appliance will slide smoothly. Just be sure to clean up the soap when you're finished.

That fresh-baked smell!

From M.R.— My secret's out! For an instant room refresher when I'm expecting company, here's what I do.

A few minutes before visitors are due to arrive I pop two slices of bread into the toaster, butter them when done and set them aside.

The house smells like fresh-baked bread. I'm always hearing, "Your place smells so good. . . ."

Later the birds get a treat.

Chapter 3

TACKLING LAUNDRY DAYS

Folks are always writing to me about laundry problems. Seems we are a nation of stain-removers, whiteners, brighteners and lint-pickers—by necessity if not by choice.

So I thought I'd open this chapter with some laundry ABCs that bear repeating. Here they are:

Sort lights from darks, delicates from sturdy fabrics. Separate lint givers from lint takers. Empty pockets. Close zippers and hooks. Check for spots and stains, and pretreat as necessary. Measure soap and detergent carefully. Choose the right washing cycle.

And when you lay your head on freshly laundered sheets smelling sweet as sunshine, sleep tight.

—HELOISE

PREPARING THE WASH

Sock trick

The way to get around sock sorting is not to have to do it.

Invest in a package of medium-sized safety pins. Each time you or someone in your family takes off a pair of socks, pin the tops together before tossing the pair into the hamper.

You'll never have to sort socks again.

Sorting system

Are you often faced with mountains of unsorted soiled laundry on washday? Here's a way to get around that awful sorting task—but everyone in the family has to help.

Make half a dozen or so laundry bags out of nylon net. Label each bag or the hook on which you hang it: whites, darks, pastels, delicates, towels—whatever categories are convenient for you.

Then sort things as they are used. As each bag fills, a load will be ready for the washer.

And if you need to wash one item in a hurry—say a favorite pair of jeans—you won't have to go through all the dirty laundry to find it.

If you don't have the space at home for such an elaborate system, try this scaled-down version. Use

51

the hamper for only large items (towels, jeans, etc.) and a laundry bag beside it for small stuff. You'll be that much ahead on washday.

A neat hamper

From W.M.— Piled up dirty laundry always frustrated me. But not any more.

Now I fold my dirty laundry and stack it in the hamper. A folded towel or sheet takes up much less space, leaving room for more shirts, etc.

And what a lift on washday! Makes my laundry look like less of a job.

Laundry reminder

From N.O.— Often I want to wash a garment but don't want to crumple it in the hamper till the next time I run the washing machine. So I jot down the name of the item on a slip of paper and drop the note in the hamper.

Next washday the note is there, reminding me to retrieve the item from drawer or closet.

Supply chest

From V.V.— We found a great place to keep all the laundry supplies in our small apartment: inside the washing machine!

That way I have lots more under-the-sink room and never have to see the detergent, fabric softener, etc. except when the machine is in use.

Spot marker

It's so frustrating to remember after you've tossed an item into the wash that it had a spot or stain that needed special treatment beforehand—even more annoying when the spot can't be found once the article is wet.

A good way to remind yourself of pre-wash chores is to pin a safety pin over a stained area. The shiny pin should catch your eye as you sort the wash, and it will help you locate a stain on a wet garment.

Pre-wash signal

From R.E.B.— I was always "setting" stains in clothing because no one in the family had told me that an item needed pre-treating before washing. Finally I came up with a solution.

Now everyone draws my attention to a stained article of clothing by tying it in a loose knot before putting it in the hamper.

Soon as I see a knot, it takes no time at all to find the spot and treat it.

AT THE LAUNDROMAT

Disposable measuring cup

From M.A.— I have to use a coin-operated laundromat. I don't like guessing how much liquid or powdered detergent I need per load, but I got tired of taking measuring cups to the laudromat and leaving them there.

So I decided to make my own. Now I save 8-ounce yogurt containers. I rinse them out, use my regular plastic measuring cup to find the quarter-cup and half-cup points on the containers, and mark them with a laundry pen.

Now if I leave my homemade measuring cup at the laundromat, it doesn't cost me anything to replace it with another.

Magnetic wash

From S.F.— When I do my laundry at a busy laundromat, it is quite a job to remember which are my washers or dryers since I usually can't get several machines in a row.

I finally thought of buying a set of colored magnets to mark my washers and dryers.

Easy to slip on the machines and easy to remove!

Time organizer

It's a real nuisance at the laundromat to keep jumping up to see if the light has gone out on a machine signaling that the wash or the drying is done.

Why not take your kitchen timer with you—or one of the new inexpensive watches with an alarm—set it accordingly, then read a magazine or write a letter without distraction?

WASHDAY KNOWHOW

How to wash a washer

If you live in a hard-water area and the inside of your washing machine has acquired a dingy coating, here's how to get it shining again.

Fill the washer with hot water and pour in a gallon of distilled vinegar. Let the washer run through its regular cycle—with no clothes in it, of course.

The solution will wash away the residue of minerals and detergent powder.

Give your washer this vinegar treatment every six months or so and you'll be delighted with how sparkling it stays.

Your clothes will smell good, too.

Douse those suds

When you accidently dump too much detergent in your washer and the machine oversuds, just sprinkle some soap granules into the water. In a few seconds the suds will disappear.

Or you can drop a bar of soap into the washer water. If you have a lint filter atop the agitator, you can put the bar in it. Either way, be sure to remove the bar of soap as soon as the suds disappear.

Detergent comes first

From A.H.— As a home economist, I am a little surprised at how many homemakers don't know it is incorrect to put clothes in the washing machine and then add the detergent.

The detergent should be added to the water first and allowed to mix well with the water before the clothes are added.

The reason for this, of course, is to have the detergent dissolved and distributed in the water so no lumps will be concentrated on the clothes.

In a concentrated form, detergent is strong and could harm the fibers in fabrics.

"Balloon" burster

Have you ever lifted the lid of your top-loading washer and watched your sheets, captured in their own air bubbles, swirling around above the suds like so many balloons?

Here's a way to avoid those "balloons."

Let the the washer fill and begin to agitate. Then "thread" in your sheets, starting from corners, and let the agitating action suck them down.

It's weird! The sheets slink into the washer all by themselves, and they agitate without air locks.

(Be sure to add pillow cases from their closed ends.)

This method also works for beach towels, bedspreads, curtains, and heavy clothing like men's trousers.

Throw in the cup

After measuring liquid detergent for the laundry in a plastic cup, be sure to rinse the cup in the wash water, or just throw the cup in with the clothes.

Not a drop of detergent will be wasted.

Laundering down articles

Drycleaning a down jacket or pillow is an expensive proposition, so washing down articles at home is an attractive alternative. Takes a little effort, though.

Here's what to do. Be sure to check seams and ticking first, then wash a down item on the delicate cycle of your machine in lukewarm to cool water with a mild soap.

Don't use a detergent; its wetting action could destroy the down's loft.

Rinse well and then press out any excess moisture by hand.

You can tumble-dry a down jacket or pillow on low or the cool cycle of your machine. But be sure to throw in a couple of tennis balls or a pair of clean sneakers with the down article. That way it will come out fluffy, not lumpy.

Also, a clean dry bath towel in the dryer will absorb any excess moisture.

Check the item periodically as it dries and gently pull apart any clumps by hand. Then return the item to the dryer.

Do not use fabric softener.

Laundering an electric blanket

Washing electric blankets isn't really difficult. After all, most are made so they can be washed. But a few precautions are indicated.

First, always be sure you have disconnected the electrical control. (Wouldn't you feel silly to find the cord in the washer, ruined?) Second, give the blanket a good shake, outside if possible, to remove any dust.

Now wash in warm water with a mild detergent. Fill the machine, let it agitate so the detergent dissolves, then place the blanket in the water and let it wash three or four minutes at most. After the water drains, follow with a short spin cycle. Rinse again and spin briefly again so that only part of the water is removed. Press the remaining water out with your hands. (Long wash or spin cycles may damage the blanket.)

Drape the balnket outdoors over two parallel lines. NEVER, NEVER, put an electric blanket in a dryer as it can damage the wiring.

Also, never run one through a coin-operated dry cleaning machine as the solvent could damage the wiring, which could result in electrical shock when in use.

If you prefer, you can take the blankets to a professional cleaner. He knows just how to care for them down to the last little bit of fluff.

Brightening synthetic whites

When dacron, nylon and other no-iron white garments turn yellow or tattletale gray, you can restore them in a bath of dishwasher detergent. That's right, *dishwasher* detergent.

Instead of laundry detergent, add the required measure of dishwasher detergent to your clothes washer.

You'll be amazed and delighted by the results.

Cheerful blacks and blues

Why have tired-looking jeans and dusty black or navy cotton dresses when it's so easy to put old-fashioned bluing in the rinse water?

Bluing will keep these dark garments—and tee-shirts and slips—a true black or navy blue.

Quilting protector

When machine washing quilted clothing, such as bathrobes, hostess gowns and children's jackets, put the quilted item in a pillow case or nylon bag to protect the stitching from the agitator of the machine.

That way there won't be the usual broken and pulled threads that make even a new article look worn out.

Shirt tip

When washing shirts and blouses, especially those of no-iron material, button up the fronts before putting articles in the water.

Button only the top three buttons if a shirt is to be hung (leaving room to slip in a hanger from the bottom). Button all the buttons if the shirt is to be folded.

Your shirts and blouses will come out of the wash cleaner and will dry smoother.

Fabric softener do's and don'ts

Do use softener to avoid static cling in synthetic items.

Don't pour liquid softener directly into the wash. It can stain clothing. Instead, if your washer doesn't have a softener dispenser, dilute the softener in a quart of water before adding it to the rinse water.

Use softeners only occasionally with fluffy things like towels. Used too often, softener makes fabrics lose absorbency.

Fabric softener substitute

If you unexpectedly run out of fabric softener you can always use creme rinse (for the hair) in its place. Just mix a capful or tablespoonful or two in a quart of water and add to the rinse water.

Of course, creme rinse is too expensive, ounce for ounce, for regular laundry use, but it's a great substitute in a pinch. Especially nice for lingerie. Makes things smell so good.

Homemade softener sheet

If you prefer liquid softener but sometimes forget to add it to the wash, just make your own softener sheet.

Wet and wring out a clean washcloth. Pour a little liquid softener on it, rub it in, and toss the cloth into the dryer with the rest of your wash load.

DRYING THE WASH

Double spin

Here's an energy saver.

When you have washed a heavy load of laundry—towels, for example, or cotton underwear—reset the washing machine after the cycle is complete to give the load an extra spin-dry treatment.

You will be surprised how much more water comes out.

With the laundry drier to start, less drying time is needed whether you machine or air-dry the things.

And if you do use a machine, you save money on your electric bill because less energy is needed to spin a washer than to spin a heat dryer.

Balancing act

Ever had your top-loading automatic washer shake and rattle to a halt trying to spin-dry one large bulky item?

Here's a way to avoid the problem.

After the wash cycle, lift the article up and center it over the top of the agitator post. All the water will spin out without affecting the balance of the machine.

Replace the article in the bottom of the washer tub for the rinse cycle, then drape it over the agitator once again for the last spin dry.

Takes a little extra attention, but this method is terrific for things that must be washed alone, such as children's bulky jackets, heavy bath rugs, mats, blankets and so on.

Winter washline (1)

From R.C.— My wife likes to hang the freshly laun-

dered wash outside even in winter. And we all love
that fresh air-dried scent.

But hanging up wet clothes in cold weather is
bone chilling work. Hands aching cold—brrrr!

The secret in our house is to do most of the job
indoors.

Shake out the wet wash inside. Open each garment and lay it flat in the laundry basket ready to
hang. Then when you step outside you can pin away
quickly.

You'll spend a minimum of time in the cold.

Winter washline (2)

Here's another way to keep hands warm while hanging out wash in cold weather:

Fill a pan with hot water and put on your rubber
gloves. Take the pan with you to the clothesline. As
your hands get chilled, dip them in the hot water.
Refill the pan with hot water as necessary.

This technique is also helpful when working outside on your car.

Wrong is right

From C.G.— I hang my laundry outdoors whenever possible. Everything smells so good!

I noticed, though, that colors were fading some-
what on the outsides of garments, but the undersides of the hems retained their color.

Now I turn everything wrong side out before
hanging and have no washed-out-looking clothes.

Give a shake

Take the time when placing wet wash in the dryer to
shake out each towel, shirt, pair of briefs, etc.

The clothes will dry faster because the air will

circulate better, and there will be fewer wrinkles.

You'll save on two energy bills—the machine's, because it runs for less time, and yours, because you don't have to iron as many things.

Drying precaution

From E.F.— After many frustrating times redrying small articles caught in the middle of a bed sheet or towel in my dryer, I discovered that if I shook out all the lumps and twists in the clothing as I put it in the dryer and—now, this is the trick—placed the smaller articles in the bottom of the dryer and the larger articles on top, my problem was solved.

I shake out the sheets, fold them crosswise and gather them loosely at the fold, and then lay them on top of one of the articles.

Everything comes out dry.

Iron with the wind

Here's a little hint for those who like to hang their clothes outside on a breezy, sunny day.

Be sure that the opening of every garment faces the wind. The garment will billow like a sail as the wind pushes the lighter back of a shirt or jacket, say, away from the heavier placket front.

You'll be amazed at how much "ironing" the wind does.

Quick indoor drying

When you hang up wet wash to dry in the basement, turn on a fan to circulate the air. The clothes will dry in half the time.

No-iron drying

Dry your no-iron shirts and blouses upside down on the clothesline.

The weight of the water will smooth out the collar and the upper part of the garment. No need to worry about the tail because that gets tucked into skirt or trousers.

HAND WASHING

Help for hand-washed sweaters

Hand-washing sweaters sure does make them smell sweet and saves a bundle on dry cleaning. But it's such a nuisance having to wring them gently by hand, then roll them in a towel, then lay them flat, etc.—the way the labels often advise—to prevent their stretching out of shape.

So here's a way around all that.

If you have a washing machine, just drop your dripping wet hand-washed sweaters into the machine, dial "damp dry" or the last spin cycle, and let the machine spin away the water. Even a minute in the machine should remove enough water to make for easy handling.

Your sweaters will come out ready to shape and to dry anywhere.

More help for hand-washed sweaters

If you like to hand-wash sweaters but don't have a washing machine at home for spinning out the rinse water, this tip will make the job a bit easier.

After washing, place the item in a large kitchen colander for rinsing. Just turn on the water and let it run through the sweater. Let stand a few minutes. Gravity will drain a lot of the water away.

Then gently squeeze out as much remaining water as you can through the colander. At least you won't have wrung-out sleeves falling back into the sink and soaking up the water squeezed out of the body.

Scrub mat

From E.J.— Many times when doing hand laundry there's a need for a little rubbing around collars and such.

I flip over my rubber sink mat and use the grooved undersides like an old-fashioned scrub board. Works just fine.

IRONS AND IRONING

How to clean an iron

If there's a buildup of gunk on the bottom of your iron, don't despair and don't try to remove it with ordinary household cleansers.

Go to a large fabric store and buy a tube of iron cleaner. That's right, there's special stuff for cleaning irons. It's very inexpensive because it lasts and lasts.

Follow directions on the tube and your ironing problems will be gone as fast as the gunk on the bottom of the iron. Don't throw away the cloth you use. Fasten it to the tube with a rubber band and just add a little more of the cleaner to it from time to time. Stretches the tube even further.

Clogged iron

When your steam iron stops putting out steam, the iron is probably clogged with lime from using hard water.

Pour full-strength vinegar (the cheapest kind) into the iron and let it steam for about five minutes.

Unplug the iron and let it stand a while longer, then pour out the vinegar. Thoroughly rinse out the iron with clean water. You may have to use a toothpick to poke through the steam holes.

To prevent clogging, always use bottled distilled water (available in your grocery store) or save rain water and strain it before pouring it into the iron.

If you must use regular tap water, never let it remain in the iron. Always empty out any water left after ironing.

Ironing board switch

Next time you iron shirts or other large articles, turn the ironing board around and use the wide end.

You'll find that shirt fronts fit neatly over the wide end. You don't have to keep adjusting a shirt to do the job.

And the wide end offers more surface area for speedy ironing of large things like tablecloths.

Ironing caddy

Are you always looking for a place within easy reach to hang up freshly ironed shirts and settling for the kitchen doorknob?

You can set up a handy caddy near your ironing board by suspending a broom or mop handle over the back of two chairs.

It's such a great convenience when you have many

items to iron and don't want to keep shuttling around
to hang things up.

Heat miser

To save electricity when ironing, do the articles that
need high heat first. Then turn down your iron and
do the low-heat things.

Last of all, unplug the iron and do the items that
call for a cool iron.

Ironing tips

With "natural fibers" blooming all over the place,
cotton shirts and shirtwaist dresses that need ironing
are making a comeback. Here are some tips for
doing a good ironing job and lightening the chore a
bit.

Iron shirts and shirtwaist dresses in approximately
the same manner. If there are cuffs, iron the insides
of them first, then the outsides. Iron the placket of
the sleeve, then the sleeve.

Next, iron the inside front facings—the button
side should be placed on a terry towel for a smoother
finish. The underside of the collar and insides of
pockets come next.

Now we're to the outside of the shirt. Starting
with the collar, iron it from the points to the center.
Yokes and shoulders should be pressed from center
back, over the shoulder, to the front of the shirt.

After pressing the back, press the two front panels.
In the case of a shirtwaist dress, iron the skirt last.

Toddler sleeve

To iron the sleeves of small children's dress shirts
and blouses, slip a half-used roll of paper towels into
the sleeves. Then press.

A great help for special-occasion clothes.

Puffy sleeves

From A.J.B.— Puffy sleeves are a torture to iron. Here's a trick I learned when my daughters were young.

Turn on a lamp with a low-wattage bulb and let it heat up. Then put the sleeve over the bulb and "iron" away by working the sleeve back and forth.

Not only will the wrinkles come out but you won't be left with a crease in the sleeve.

Speedy ironing

When you are in a hurry and need to iron just one piece of clothing, don't bother to pull out your ironing board.

Instead use your kitchen cutting board. Cover it with a cushioning towel and then a pillowcase. Then iron away.

You can also set up a towel and pillowcase "board" on the floor.

Smooth trousers

When ironing trousers, pull the pockets inside out so their impression won't be left on the cloth.

Hand protector

When you have a large load of ironing to do, wrap the handle of your iron in an old nylon stocking. You'll avoid blisters and aching hands.

Bumpy stuff

Here's a way to iron eyelets, embroidery, crocheted doilies and other bumpy stuff so the knobby side fluffs up.

Spray starch on the right side, then place the

article right side down on a terry towel and iron on the wrong side.

That way the starch doesn't get on the iron. And when you turn over the eyelet collar, doily or whatever, the knobs and stitches stand up.

REMOVING STAINS

First law of stain removal

Whatever solvent you are using—alcohol, vinegar, hair spray, you name it—always test a hidden piece of fabric—a seam, for instance—before you proceed.

You never know when a color might run or fade.

Second law of stain removal

Remember always to work from the back or underside of a stain and place some absorbent material underneath.

When you apply solvent to the back, you force the stain out the way it came in, rather than more deeply into the fabric.

Spotter's trick

From C.R.— Here's a tip from an old hand in the cleaning business.

Always apply cleaning solvent around a spot, not on it. Then, using a small brush, stroke the solvent towards the center of the spot, blotting as you go with a paper towel.

Take care not to brush through the spot for that would spread the diluted stain outward, making the spot larger.

Mechanic's secret

From D.J.C.— When clothes get oil-based stains, one of the best treatments around is waterless hand cleaner. This cream-type cleaner is available at any automotive supply store and also at hardware stores.

Spread a dollop of the cleaner over the stain and rub it in with an old toothbrush or clean cloth. Leave the cream on the garment for about 20 minutes, then wash the garment by itself.

Waterless hand cleaner won't remove every oil stain but it can rescue some badly soiled items.

Grease remedy

A simple home remedy for removing some grease spots from clothing is to apply baby powder or other talc to the spot.

Leave it on for at least two hours, then use a dry, clean toothbrush to remove the powder, brushing lightly, so as not to mar the nap of the fabric.

If the spot is not completely removed, repeat the process.

Removing orange-colored stains

Orange stains—the ones that spaghetti sauce and French salad dressing leave—sure are a nuisance. Especially when you stain a garment while dining out.

But there's an easy remedy that you can take immediately.

Dampen a cotton napkin (or washcloth) in water, wring it out and squeeze lemon juice (or white vinegar) on it. Dampening first allows the lemon juice to be absorbed into the napkin. Then take the lemon-soaked cloth, blot that ugly orange stain and watch it disappear. Then rinse in clear water.

This method works beautifully on synthetic-fiber (no silk please) and drip-dry clothes as well as cottons.

Makeup stains

Use pure white vinegar to remove face powder and cake makeup stains from the collar of synthetic-fiber blouses and dresses.

Just dip a *dry* white terry washcloth in pure white vinegar and wring out well. Rub the soiled spot and let dry.

The vinegar odor will disappear when the spot is dry.

Lipstick remover (1)

Did you know that rubbing alcohol will remove most (but not all) lipstick stains from clothing?

Place the stained article over something absorbent, pour a little alcohol over the stain, then rub with a cotton ball doused in alcohol. It works beautifully.

Lipstick remover (2)

Here's how to remove lipstick stains from your good cloth napkins: Treat them with shampoo. That's right, the stuff you wash your hair with.

Just rub a little shampoo into each stain, let stand 20 minutes, then wash as usual. It usually does the trick.

Removing blood stains

An effective remedy for blood stains, both fresh stains and dried ones, is unseasoned meat tenderizer.

Wet the stained area with cold water and lay it over paper towels. Sprinkle the stain with tenderizer. Let it stand a few moments, then take an old toothbrush and brush until the blood disappears into the towel. Wash the garment as usual.

The ball point "blues"

Ball point ink stains have everyone singing the blues at one time or another. There's nothing like a leaky pen to ruin a garment or upholstery.

Since there are many kinds of ball point inks, removing a ball point stain takes a bit of experimenting. You never know what remedy will get out the ink. Here are a few suggestions.

First, test the solvent in a hidden place—open a hem if you have to. You don't have anything to lose once a garment is badly stained with ink.

Then try treating the stain with hair spray. Just spray it on and rub in with a soft cloth. With luck the ink mark will disappear.

You can also try plain rubbing alcohol. It often does the trick.

Another remedy is one of the commercial pre-wash sprays on the market today. Follow directions on the container.

If you know what pen caused an ink stain, use it to mark a rag of similar fabric. Then test the solvents on the rag stain before you treat the garment. That way you don't have to subject a garment to several solvents to discover which one works.

Scorch standby

On clothing scorched by ironing, try a treatment of plain 3-percent hydrogen peroxide.

Apply a little at a time with a cotton ball, taking care the peroxide doesn't damage the fabric. Rub gently, then lay a clean white facial tissue or cotton

handkerchief over the scorch and iron. That brown
scorch spot should disappear.

Rust remover

Rust stains in clothing and tablecloths can be removed by a sprinkle of salt moistened with lemon
juice, followed by drying in the sun.

Don't ever use liquid bleach on rust spots. The
rust actually speeds up the action of the bleach and
may cause a hole in the fabric.

REMOVING LINT

Lint picker

A very fine crochet hook neatly removes the lint and
dust that often accumulate under the cloth around
button and collar tabs and inside plackets and cuffs.

Just gently poke a hole through the facing and pull
out the lint collection, and that dingy look will disappear from light-colored clothing.

Lint lifter

Ever drop the cuffs on a pair of trousers or rip the
hem of a dress and find a nasty trail of lint along the
crease?

A square of nylon net will easily lift the lint away
so you can press out the crease.

Four-way refresher

A cup of white vinegar added to the final rinse water
of your wash helps remove lint from clothes, especially dark ones.

The vinegar also brightenes colors, deodorizes

the clothing and even cleans the washing machine. What a welcome addition to your laundry supply shelf!

Lint sweeper

From J.W.— When I need to brush away lint from dark clothing and there's no clothes brush handy, I use a plastic credit card.

I "sweep" the cloth with the edge of the card. That generates static electricity so the lint (and pet hair, too) clings to the card. Then I sweep the card with thumb and forefinger and dispose of the lint.

This trick really comes in handy when I'm traveling.

Disposable lint can

Use an old detergent box to hold the little "blankets" of lint removed from your dryer's lint trap. When the box is full, throw the whole thing away.

Lint discouragers

Annoying lint on freshly washed dark and colored clothing can drive anyone up the laundry room wall. So here are some tips for avoiding lint.

First, don't wash your dark things after you have done the rest of the laundry. Do the darks first. Lint from bath towels and cottons can cling to washer and dryer tubs after the cycle is over.

If you do your laundry at a laundromat, wipe out the washer and dryer with damp paper towels before you put your dark garments in. Who knows, some person before you might have washed and dried a shag rug!

Another way to eliminate lint is always to turn your garments wrong side out. They will get just as clean. Besides, most body oils and perspiration accumulate on the insides of clothes.

Then, too, the outsides of garments turned inside out for washing and drying will stay new looking longer because they do not receive so much friction from the machines.

Goodbye fuzzies

Before you throw out that sweater covered with ugly "pills" or fuzz, try shaving it—yes, shaving it, with a razor.

Lay the sweater flat on a table or your ironing board. Hold the fabric taut and lightly shave the surface, taking care not to nick the fabric.

The results will amaze you—a new-looking sweater!

Laundry care labels

Those little care instruction labels in blouses, shirts and other tops can really irritate the back of your neck. But if you tear them out, you can easily forget whether an item should be hand-washed, washed in cold water or dry-cleaned.

So here's the Heloise system for keeping necks happy and washing care instructions in order.

As soon as you get home with a new garment, check the label. If it says machine wash, rip or snip that offending label right out.

When washday arrives, if there's no care tag in the garment, you know it is to be machine washed.

As for labels you want to leave in, trim the corners or rub with a fabric softener sheet to cut down on scratchiness.

Chapter 4

IN THE KITCHEN

For me the kitchen is the heart of the home. I live and work in one big rambling place but so long as the kitchen is under control I can get on with the rest of the day's occupations.

That's why I get such a kick out of all the "kitchen capers" and storage tips and other hints that you'll find in this chapter.

Every time I snag a bargain, save a burned dish, flip a bread wrapper or do something "the easy way" to keep that kitchen "smiling," I smile too.

And I hope you do.

—Hugs, HELOISE

SHOPPING SAVVY

Cashing in your coupons

Buy the large economy packets of standard sized envelopes, and use them for grocery lists. After each trip to the store, attach an envelope to a magnetic clip and hang it on your refrigerator door.

As you realize the need for an item, write it on the envelope front and immediately tuck a corresponding "cents-off" coupon (if you have one) inside the envelope. When it's time to shop, put the envelope in your purse or pocket, and you're off.

This will help tremendously in organizing shopping. No longer will you find yourself struggling at the last minute to sort out necessary coupons. Don't you often find that the very ones you want seem to have disappeared?

The clip-on envelope method cures all that. You will be using more coupons than ever before—and that means savings.

Efficiency in the aisles

Organize your grocery list by the order in which you find things in the aisles. Or set up your list by category —produce, paper goods, etc. Wherever you shop you won't waste time doubling back to the same aisle.

Efficient grocery shopping

A small clipboard (about 5 by 8 inches) is a great help when shopping for groceries.

Clip your shopping list and any coupons you intend using onto the board before going to the store.

The board gives a firm backing to check off items on your list, and you don't have to rummage in your purse or pocket for the coupons.

Also keep a piece of blank paper under your list for quick figuring or noting prices for future reference.

Coupon clipper

Here is an idea for a handy and safe clipper for coupons and newspaper items.

Save the spent cartridge in which double-edged stainless steel razor blades come.

Then slip an old or used blade back into the spring-loaded cartridge.

To use—just hold the cartridge and, with the thumb, slip the blade *halfway* out so the cutting edge is exposed. Then cut away.

When through using, just slip the blade back in.

Plastic bag opener

Opening those plastic produce bags dispensed on a roll at the supermarket sure can be a nuisance.

But there's a simple remedy for a stuck opening. Just rub the top of the bag across your arm and it will open easily.

Use your head

Ever struggle to get a head of lettuce into a plastic produce bag?

Well, next time don't put the lettuce in the bag.

Put the bag over the lettuce. Simply place your hand inside the plastic sack, grab the head of lettuce, cabbage, or whatever, and pull the sack over the vegetable.

So easy.

How to pick a melon

Here's a guide to picking the best melon for your money.

Cantaloupes should be tan in color, no green showing through. Green means green! The end should be soft and the cantaloupe smell should be strong and delicious. (You can detect the aroma much better when the fruit is at room temperature.)

Ripe honeydew melons, when shaken, should make a sloshing sound caused by the seeds and juice.

When squeezed, a ripe papaya should feel "rubbery." If it isn't ripe when opened, just put the halves back together and leave the fruit out of the refrigerator for a day or two.

As for watermelon, don't be bashful. Thump vigorously on several of those green gourds. The one with the most hollow sound is the ripest.

STORAGE TIPS

Two-for-one bottle

Cut a plastic two-liter soft drink bottle in half and you get two handy items. The top makes a funnel with an extra big spout, and the bottom makes a tall canister for storing carrot sticks and celery sticks upright in the fridge.

Just cover the canister with a plastic lid from some

other container or a piece of plastic wrap, and the vegetables will stay fresh and crisp for several days.

Vegetable keeper

The bottom of a gallon plastic milk jug also makes a good vegetable keeper. Slice through the plastic jug about four inches from the bottom.

Great for keeping your refrigerator's vegetable drawer neat.

Vegetable saver

If you do not use fresh vegetables soon after purchasing them, they may rot in the moisture that forms inside their plastic bag.

To prevent this, wrap a sheet or two of paper toweling loosely around the vegetables. If humidity is high, use two thicknesses. The vegetables do not have to be completely covered with the paper towel, as it is there just to absorb moisture.

Replace the vegetables, towel and all, back in the bag, and close with a twistie.

Cut-side cover

Don't throw away those small pieces of paper used to separate individual slices of cheese. Clip them together and use them to cover the cut side of a tomato, lemon, or whatever, before placing it in the fridge.

Saves using up the plastic wrap on the roll.

Bottoms up!

The refrigerator shelf life of many foods is extended by storing them upside down. Turning a container upside down prevents air from entering the lid and encouraging the growth of microorganisms.

For example, cottage cheese and sour cream will stay mold-free longer if turned topsy-turvy after the first opening. Just make sure the lids are on tight!

Relish, pickes and other foods packed in vinegar will also keep better. That white stuff called "mother" that often forms on the surface will not appear.

Tips for opening jars

If you have trouble opening twist-type jar covers, here's some help:

Put a rubber band around the lid for a surer grip. Then twist.

Jars to be refrigerated should be opened *before* chilling. They open more easily at room temperature.

Try slipping a plastic sandwich bag or a piece of plastic wrap over the top of a jar once you have opened it. Replace the cover and next time it will twist off easily.

Non-slip jars

Wrap the necks of slippery jars and bottles with several rubber bands. That way a cold, wet container won't slide out of your hands.

Take this lying down

Store almost empty jars of jam, mayonnaise, mustard, relish, etc., on their sides.

Makes it so much easier to scrape out that last little bit without wasting any.

Creating a vacuum

To prolong freshness when freezing food in a plastic bag, it's best to remove all the air before sealing.

To do this, immerse the filled bag in water before

sealing, taking care not to let any water enter the bag. The pressure of the water will force any air out of the bag. Now seal promptly.

Pick a bag

From L.M.F.— One of my kitchen drawers was overflowing with plastic bread wrappers and produce bags. I hate to throw away perfectly good bags, but they were getting to be a nuisance.

So I stuffed them into an empty decorative facial tissue box. A single bag pulls out easily and now my cluttered drawer is free to hold other things.

Container switch

How difficult it can be to pour thick salad dressing out of those silly narrow-necked bottles.

To get around that, as soon as you open a bottle just invert it and place it in a plastic container such as the tubs whipped topping comes in.

Leave the bottle propped up in the container for about 20 minutes. You'll be surprised how the dressing all drains out.

Keep the dressing in the covered container and spoon it on your salads as needed.

First in, first out

From J.S.— As a nurse I deal with dated drugs and supplies. As new ones are received, they are placed at the back or at the bottom of the stack so the older ones may be used first.

I adopted this procedure at home. I put new canned goods at the back of the shelf and fresh supplies of meat on the bottom of the drawer in the refrigerator. I leave eggs in the carton until those in the egg container are used, etc.

That way, older purchases are always used first.

Dating system

From G.R.— When canned items I like are on sale at the grocery, I buy in quantity.

I use a large marking pencil and write the date of purchase on the top of each can.

If the cans get pushed around in the cupboard, I can quickly find out which were purchased earliest and use them up first.

You can do it

It is easier to stack canned foods if you put a piece of light cardboard between the stacks.

That way the cans in the top row sit on their own "shelf" and do not fall over so easily.

Stacking slickly

Cupboard space—or rather lack of it—is one of the big problems in many kitchens.

Do you know this trick? Place a paper doily between two glasses. Then they can be stacked without danger of sticking together.

Stacking does save space and every little bit helps.

Another thing you can do is place a square of waxed paper between two glasses. That lets them slide on and off—or is it in and out?—quite easily.

Space economy

Does it seem like you never have enough room to put away all the glasses?

If some of your glasses are larger on top than on the bottom, or vice versa, try turning every other glass upside down on the shelf.

This works well with wine glasses and tapered or odd-shaped glasses.

Saves a lot of space. Often you can get almost twice as many on the shelf.

Blender bender

From M.M.C.— Whenever I used my blender, I found it difficult to unscrew the bottom assembly that holds the rubber washer and blades.

My 14-year-old son saw me struggling one day and came to the rescue. He set the glass container, with the bottom assembly attached, back into the blender base, grabbed the handle on the blender container and turned counterclockwise slightly. The bottom assembly loosened enough to unscrew easily. No more struggling.

Sugar storage

No, you do not have to dash a package of sugar on the floor when it gets hard. Don't let it get hard.

Tie up a newly purchased sack of sugar in a plastic bag, for storage. When you do open the bag, transfer all the sugar to a clean, dry plastic milk jug.

Pouring from the jug is easy and the sugar will not harden in it.

Shake it!

Save those empty spice and meat tenderizer jars that come with perforated inner lids.

Great for dispensing your own cinnamon and sugar mixture or vinegar for salads.

Storing brown sugar

There's a simple way to keep brown sugar from getting hard.

After opening a box of brown sugar, place the box inside a plastic bag, then seal the bag tightly with a twistie or use a self-sealing bag. The sugar will stay soft on your cupboard shelf—it doesn't have to be refrigerated.

To soften brown sugar already hard and lumpy, place the sugar in a baking pan, then set it in a warm oven for a few minutes. Stir the sugar frequently and leave it in the oven only until it is softened. Place it in a plastic bag to store.

It will stay soft and moist almost indefinitely so none will go to waste.

KITCHEN CAPERS

Paraffin heater

Here's a tip for those who do a lot of canning.

Make a paraffin-heating container out of a clean No. 2 can. To make a pouring spout, flatten opposite sides of the can by pressing them together.

Put the paraffin in the can and set the can in a small pan of water an inch or so deep. Heat until the paraffin has melted.

Saves having to wipe out the top of your double boiler. And the container can be used indefinitely.

Paraffin lifter

Ever grappled with the paraffin cover to a jar of preserves and been reduced to smashing it with a knife handle and then fishing out the paraffin pieces? Relief is at hand.

Before pouring paraffin over filled jars of jam or jelly, place a loop of clean string (about 6 to 10 inches long) over the top of the preserves. Let the ends hang over the sides of the jar. Then pour in the paraffin.

After the paraffin has hardened, the string serves as a lifter for removing it. Just grip the two ends of string and gently tug. The paraffin plug will emerge neatly.

No spilled preserves. And no paraffin floating in the jam.

The trick is especially helpful when using glass jars with openings narrower than the body of the jar.

Easy sterilizing

If you have a dishwasher, usually you can heat your canning jars in it to sterilize them, as long as the water temperature is hot enough. But if you don't have a dishwasher or it is not convenient to use when you need it, try the oven method.

First rinse the jars in very hot water from the faucet. Line your oven grate with aluminum foil and set the jars upside down on the covered grate. Turn the oven to 150 degrees. Heat the jars for ten minutes.

The jars are now ready for use when you are ready to fill them.

Stuck glass

From N.W.— Somehow, while washing the dishes, I managed to get a cut-glass drinking glass wedged into a large mug. Putting them back into the soapy water didn't help.

Then I dried off the stuck items as best I could, trickled a little cooking oil in between the two and filled the glass with ice cubes.

I waited a few minutes and voilà—the glass slipped out as smooth as silk.

Glue residue

Plastic drinking glasses and cups often come with a price sticker glued to the surface. If you soak them in hot water the paper will come off, but the sticky glue may remain.

To remove that ornery glue, sprinkle cornmeal or baking soda on the sticky residue and rub, rub, rub with a dry cloth, adding more cornmeal or soda as necessary.

This will not mar the finish of the plastic as so many things you might use would do, yet it is very effective.

Plasticware care

To remove stickiness from plasticware, make a paste of baking soda and water, then rub it on the affected pieces.

This works particularly well on those containers used to carry salad dressings, when hot sudsy water alone doesn't do the trick.

Also, to remove an unpleasant odor from plasticware, put a piece of crumpled newspaper or a piece of activated charcoal in the container and put the cover on. Leave on overnight.

Plasticware cleaner

From D.J.— I use a prewash spray stain remover in a pressurized can to clean sticky plastic containers, then follow with the usual washing in detergent.

The containers come out like new. All sticky film is removed.

Pest control (1)

From E.W.— When I opened my sugar canister

one day, I saw a lot of ants in it. I quickly clamped the lid on, lest they run all over the kitchen, and then had the notion to shove the canister in the freezer.

When I removed the canister a couple of hours later, the ants were all in a cluster on top of the sugar. Good and dead.

An effective method, for sure. What one does with sugar or whatever is a private matter!

Pest control (2)

From M.H.— We've all been plagued by those pesky little sugar ants in kitchen cupboards and cabinets and on counter tops. They are tough. Those commercial poison traps don't seem to work well.

Recently I heard that wiping down surfaces with white vinegar gets rid of the critters. I wiped down every surface I could and after four days the coast was clear.

Microwaving tip

When warming or sautéing certain foods in the microwave, try using a cheap paper plate to cover the dish.

The paper plate will not go limp and fall into the food as do paper towels, waxed paper, etc.

Getting out the fat (1)

From V.G.— After cooking a delicious roast beef, I wanted to drain off the fat before cooking vegetables in the broth.

Rather than placing the broth in the refrigerator for the long process of cooling to congeal the fat at the top so I could skim it off, I dropped a few ice cubes in.

Imagine my surprise to see the grease cling to those ice cubes like iron to a magnet. All I had to do was dip out the fat-clad cubes and proceed with my broth and vegetable dish.

The water from the ice cubes did not affect the broth at all.

Getting out the fat (2)

A quick way to remove greasy fat from meat drippings (to make gravy) after you've cooked a roast, for instance, is to set a heavy cup in a bowl or small saucepan and slowly pour the drippings into the cup.

As you pour, the stock will settle to the bottom and the grease will rise to the top of the cup and spill over. Continue pouring until only stock fills the cup. (Of course, use another cup if needed after the first one is filled with stock.)

If you don't have enough stock to fill the cup, add water as it too will sink and force the grease to spill over. (You will probably need to add water to the drippings anyway to make gravy.)

Getting out the fat (3)

From P.V. — I've hated grease in gravy ever since I was a small boy. This is how I avoid it when making roasts or whatever.

Tip the pan up to make a deep well of fluid at one end. Depress the bulb of a baster and insert the tip through the floating grease down into the meat stock.

When you release the bulb, the baster will draw up almost pure meat juice.

Repeat until most of the stock is transferred to a saucepan. The demarcation of the stock and grease is easy to see.

No-twist twistie

Sometimes twisties can be annoying. Seems that no matter which way you turn, the stubborn things snag and won't come apart.

So next time you use a twistie to close a bag or wrapper, don't twist the wire around itself. Instead, wrap the wire around the bag, making a little spiral.

Closes the bag perfectly—and to open it, you just start at either end of the spiral and unwind.

Bread-wrapper twist!

Who said you have to use a twistie or a plastic tab to close a loaf of bread?

Just take the neck of the wrapper, twist it a few times to get the air out, then pull the open end of the wrapper back down over the bread.

Now your bread is double-wrapped as well as sealed without a twistie. And that's a twist!

Wrapper shaker

Save those bread wrappers. Shake out the crumbs, then store them with your aluminum foil, sandwich bags, etc.

Bread wrappers are strong and make great bags for shaking fish, chicken, chops, and so on in bread crumbs. When you are finished, there's no mess to to clean up. Just toss the bag in the garbage.

Bread-wrapper flour board

When making piecrust, cookies, etc., you can roll out your dough on a long plastic bread wrapper instead of the customary wax paper. Simply dampen the counter top well, then smooth out the wrapper on it.

Wax paper may move around or tear—but not plastic! And the best part is that it's free!

Oil bottle collar

You can readily solve the problem of the drippy, messy vegetable oil bottle.

Each time you start a new bottle, take a piece of paper towel or clean cloth long enough to wrap around the neck of the bottle and fold it into a strip about an inch-and-a-half wide. Fasten it around the neck of the bottle with a rubber band.

The towel or cloth collar will catch drips before they run all the way down the bottle and prevent your shelf from getting gummed up.

The cut-off top of an old cotton crew sock also fills the bill.

Oil dispenser

A plastic pancake syrup bottle makes a great cooking oil dispenser.

Especially handy if you do a lot of frying and buy large unwieldly glass jugs of cooking oil.

Transfer the oil with a funnel.

Plastic wrap finder (1)

When using transparent plastic wrap, place a paper clip or a flat plastic tab under the wrap on the roll after cutting.

You'll be able to find the edge the next time you want to use the wrap.

No more frustration.

Plastic wrap finder (2)

From J.J.R.— I was having trouble finding the beginning of a new roll of plastic wrap. (This has always been a fly in my ointment!)

I took a piece of clear sticky tape and pressed against the roll, then lifted, rotated the roll slightly and repeated until I came to the loose (??) edge. It then lifted with the tape. Hallelujah.

Chill the wrap

From B.C.— I have always complained about plastic wrap tangling whenever I try to tear it off.

I learned to simply place it in the freezer and, surprise, surprise, it rolls off smooth as silk when I use it the next time.

All wrapped up

From K.F.C.— Two new uses for plastic wrap . . .

When pans need to be soaked for a while (even with a good stopper I've found the water often leaks out), place a piece of plastic wrap around the bottom of the stopper.

For a kitchen exhaust fan that needs to be covered when not in use (to keep air out), try plastic wrap. It will stick to the wall surrounding the fan.

PREPARATION POINTERS

Neater apples

When peeling apples, use a sharp knife to cut out the bloom end of the apple (opposite from the stem end) before starting to peel.

You won't have to wash gritty black pieces of bloom off the peeled fruit.

Bacon flavor

Don't throw away those paper towels or brown paper bags used to drain grease when cooking bacon. Store them in a plastic bag in the freezer.

When baking potatoes, use the paper to grease the skins. If you have a microwave, wrap each potato in a piece of towel.

Salvaging burned beans

When cooking dry beans, should the water cook out and the beans burn, don't add water to them.

Instead, just set the pan in cold water until the beans are cool. Then pour the unburned beans into another pan. Add more water and also more seasoning if desired.

They will not taste burned.

For bean lovers

If you like beans but they don't like you, put a pinch of ground ginger in the beans when cooking them. Just a pinch will do the trick.

Add the ginger to dried beans, canned beans, bean soups, chili beans or whatever. The taste can-

not be detected but it works almost like magic. Give
it a try and see for yourself. You and beans will get
along fine.

Butter dots

To "dot with butter," as casserole recipes often ask
you to do, without getting little unsightly puddles of
butter, try this:

Put a stick of butter in the freezer until the butter
is hard. Then, using the shredding side of a grater
(largest holes), simply grate bits of butter over the
entire top of the casserole.

Distributes the butter beautifully and evenly,
takes only seconds, and works like a charm.

Pan-frying with butter

Want to keep butter from burning in a skillet when
pan-frying meats?

Always put a bit of vegetable oil in the bottom of
your skillet first. As soon as it gets hot, put your dabs
of butter in. This way the butter floats on top of the
oil, bubbles up (and mixes beautifully), and browns
gently without ever burning.

Cake frosting strategy

When frosting a three-layer cake, do you have trouble with the layers slipping and sliding? Here's a way
around that.

Frost or fill the layers, stack them, and then "pin"
them with sticks of spaghetti—one at each of the
three points of an imaginary triangle. Then frost the
sides, and there you have it.

Before serving the cake, carefully remove the
spaghetti.

Just sift it!

From J.R.S.— Did you ever empty a cake mix into the mixing bowl and wonder how on earth you could ever beat out all those lumps?

I probably beat a zillion cakes to death before my 86-year-old mother-in-law came to the rescue by telling me her secret for a good cake made with a cake mix.

She simply sifts the mix and it makes all the difference in the world!

Frosting tip

Before frosting an angel food cake, chill the cake in the refrigerator. The frosting is easier to put on and no mess!

Pineapple upside-down cake

From H.D.— I make individual pineapple upside-down cakes in the little tins that pot pies come in.

Put sugar, butter and one slice of pineapple in each pan. Use a small box of cake mix and divide the batter into five or six parts depending on number of cakes you want to bake.

The cakes can be frozen, then popped into the oven and heated. A real time-saver.

Batter up!

To fill cupcake cups or papers with a minimum of dripping, use a soup ladle or a large flour scoop.

Or transfer the batter from the mixing bowl into a clean half-gallon milk carton. Open the top of the milk carton completely first.

Then close part of the top and pour from the spout portion of the carton into cupcake papers or if you prefer, right into the greased tin.

The spout of the carton works like a charm. You can stop the flow of the batter at whatever level you wish to fill the tins.

Wrapping a slice

Here's a way to wrap a piece of frosted cake so that the frosting doesn't come off when the wrap is removed.

First take a piece of plastic wrap and lightly spread it with margarine or butter; then put this greased section over the frosting. Cover with additional wrap if needed.

Great for lunch boxes!

Pound-cake reviver

Know what to do with a stale, dry-tasting pound cake? Steam it.

Take a cake or pie plate, fill it with water and set a small cake rack over it.

Put what's left of the pound cake on the cake rack and cover the whole thing well with foil so no steam will escape. Then pop it in the oven at about 200 degrees for 10 minutes or so. Then turn off the oven and let the cake steam.

It comes out nice and moist and will last a few more days.

Bouillon softener

Place a celery leaf or sprig of parsley in the bouillon cube container and the cubes will soften and stay that way for weeks.

When the leaf or sprig is dry, replace with a fresh one.

Whack that cube!

Never mind trying to dissolve bouillon cubes in boiling water.

Take a cube, still wrapped in paper and give it one good whack with a household hammer, or the side of a meat tenderizer.

Unwrap it and you have completely pulverized bouillon, ready to dissolve in whatever you are cooking.

Bouillon tip

Add a bouillon cube to creamed vegetables. Pulverize first or dissolve in a tablespoon of water.

Delicious.

Coffee spoon

Do you drink instant coffee and always buy it in large jars?

If so, put a rubber band around the jar and slip a long-handled teaspoon under the band. Now the spoon is always handy when you need it. Beats taking out a spoon to measure coffee every time you want a cup.

When the jar is half empty, put the spoon inside.

Substitute coffee filter

If you run out of filters for your coffee maker, use a sheet of nonfibrous paper toweling.

Works great in a pinch.

Well-behaved melon (1)

Like cantaloupe but not the smell it leaves in your refrigerator?

Just pop the melon into a bread wrapper, tie tightly or secure with a twistie.

Well-behaved melon (2)

To keep cantaloupe and honeydew melons from sliding about on the plate, try this:

   After slicing the melon in half (or smaller), turn
each piece over, rind side up. At the middle of each
piece, slice a thin layer of rind off. This will give the
slice a level base to sit on.

No-fail pasta cooking

For a perfect pot of pasta, follow this method:

   Use the amount of water suggested on the package, add salt and a bit of oil or butter and bring to a
boil.

   Add the pasta and stir. Bring to a hard boil, stir
once or twice with a fork, cover and remove the pot
from the heat.

   Do not remove the lid—not even to peek—for 15
to 20 minutes, and the pasta will be cooked to per-
fection—piping hot and ready to drain and serve
with your favorite sauce.

   If you have any pasta left over, put it in a container, cover with cold water then cover the container with a tight-fitting lid. It will keep nicely for
two or three days in the refrigerator.

No boil-over pasta cooking

When cooking macaroni or spaghetti, dip a piece of
paper towel in either oil or margarine and wipe it
around the top of the pot. Surprisingly, the water
will not boil over—it will boil right up to the top and
no farther.

   Sure avoids cleaning a messy stove.

Measuring peanut butter

To easily measure peanut butter for cookies, etc.

(also, to get the last drop from the jar), place the sealed jar under hot, running water.

When the peanut butter is warm and soft, it runs right out of the jar.

If you heat the measuring cup—or grease it—the measured peanut butter will transfer to the mixing bowl just as easily.

Potato science (1)

If you want to bake a potato, do not wrap it in aluminum foil. Since potatoes are mostly moisture, foil wrapping will give you a steamed, not baked, potato!

Try this some time:

Wrap one washed potato in foil. Wash, dry with a paper towel, then lightly grease the other. Bake both in the oven at the same time.

You will find a world of difference in the flavor of the two potatoes.

Potato science (2)

Don't you just hate those pithy potatoes that grow eyes?

They seem to stare you in the face, saying, "Look, go buy some new ones."

When you see little white buds growing on potatoes, take your fingernail or a knife, and pop them off!

Your potatoes won't shrink and shrivel . . . and they will keep longer.

Try it. It works.

Test it this way yourself:

Save two potatoes from the same batch. Let one grow eyes, but keep the eyes scratched off the other one.

Leave them in your potato bin for a month or so. . . . You'll see.

Leftover potatoes

Don't throw away that dollop of leftover creamed potatoes!

Refrigerate covered until the next day. Add one whole egg, enough flour to equal the potatoes, and one teaspoon baking powder.

Mix and drop by spoonfuls into hot oil. Remove when brown. Makes a quick addition to the next meal. Delicious.

Nutritious potatoes

From A.C.— You know how people are always saying when you pour the water off the potatoes you pour all the nutrients off too?

Well, our family likes mashed potatoes, so my mom boils the potatoes in only a little water, then she leaves all the water in, puts in some powdered milk and mashes it all together.

If potatoes are too stiff, add hot water. Season to taste, and you have delicious mashed potatoes with all that good nutrition left in.

Tasty potato peels

When peeling potatoes, don't throw away the peels. First, scrub the potatoes, then peel as usual.

Add a small amount of oil and salt to the peelings, spread them on pans and bake until crisp.

Drain on paper towels and they make a delicious snack. Besides that, they cost almost nothing!

No bubbling over

A bit of margarine in a pan of potatoes put on to boil will keep the potatoes from boiling over.

Energy saver

Baking meatloaf in the oven and want mashed potatoes to go with it?

Peel and prepare the potatoes as usual and put them in a covered baking dish along with your usual amount of water or just slightly less. Put the dish of potatoes in the oven with the meatloaf.

Saves energy and is convenient, too.

Potato salad tip

From N.W.— Here's my secret for keeping potato salad fresh-tasting.

Let the potatoes get completely cold before making the salad and it will be as good the second and third days as it was the first.

Also, the salad keeps better if you leave out the onions. I serve the onions in a separate bowl and let each person add them if desired.

Neat tomatoes

From M.F.C.— I've always disliked it when I sliced a tomato for a salad and the insides fell out.

So I've found a way not to lose any of the tomato! First, I slice the tomato in half through the middle. Then I set each half on end, cut side up, and slice through the solid "stripes" to make wedges.

When the wedges are extra large, they can be cut in half and they'll still remain intact.

Tomato freezing

Freeze whole tomatoes after washing and drying them. When needed, just drop the frozen tomatoes into cooked foods like soups, stews, etc.

If you freeze them whole, no juice is lost and they don't stick together.

Tomato ripener

Take those pale tomatoes you buy in fall and winter and put them under a "grow light" with your house plants.

In a day or two they look and taste almost as if they came straight from a summer garden.

Sure brightens up those winter salads.

Skinning a tomato

To make peeling a tomato easier, go over the entire tomato with the back of a paring knife. Use a scraping motion. This loosens the skin and it peels right off.

With particularly tough skins, just drop the tomatoes into boiling water for a few seconds.

The skins will then peel readily.

No-bleed tomato slices

Did you know? Tomatoes may be skinned, sliced and arranged for serving several hours in advance of meal time if you cut them up-and-down (from stem to bottom) instead of crosswise?

They don't seem to bleed their juice and seeds when done this way.

Chapter 5

AT YOUR LEISURE

Seems to me there are no sweeter pleasures than the ones we give ourselves.

It sure is a good feeling when your pet snuggles up to you at the end of the day—when your thumb finally turns green and those plants start to thrive— when you complete a sewing project and the person you made it for (maybe yourself!) models it with glee.

This chapter shares some hints for handling those labors of love so you can better enjoy the fruits!

—Hugs, HELOISE

POTS AND PLANTERS

Flower box treatment

Before planting anything in those cute wooden flower boxes, use a water seal on the insides first.

This will preserve the wood and also help prevent insects from bothering your flowers.

Soak before switching

Before transplanting a plant to a clay pot, soak the pot overnight in water.

That way the pores of the clay will soak up moisture and not take it from the soil, which would rob the plant.

How to paint a pot

When painting flower pots, turn them upside down over a can. The can should be tall enough to hold the rim of the pot above the surface of your workbench.

You can then reach all parts, protect your hands and do a neater job.

Prettying pots

One way to spruce up old clay pots is to wind them with rope twine. Here's how.

First spread white glue on the outside of the pot and about an inch down inside the rim.

Next, wind the rope twine around the pot, going from bottom to top and then down the inside for an inch. That's all.

Inexpensive—and pretty to look at!

Square safeguards

From J.H.— To protect the carpet under my flower pots I cut 9-inch squares of acrylic plastic from a large sheet purchased at the discount store.

I attach small rubber adhesive-backed protector pads under each corner to raise the squares up so that air can circulate under them.

Then I seat my flower pots on the squares atop the carpeting.

No wet carpet and no mildew!

Anchoring porch pots

Flower pots on a porch railing can be attractive. But they are easily blown over by the wind or knocked over accidentally.

This can easily be remedied by driving a three-inch-long nail part-way into the railing and then slipping the drainage hole of the pot over the rail.

You will never have any more trouble with flower-pots being knocked over.

Stop pot spots

From R.M.T.— I like the looks of clay pots in a window. But after a certain length of time ugly white spots appear on the clay.

I solved the problem by applying a light coat of vegetable oil to the outsides of my pots.

When white spots reappear, I just wipe on another coat of oil.

My terra-cotta pots always look like new.

Looks good, does good

Another treatment for terra-cotta pots—both new ones and renovated ones—is a coat of redwood stain on the outside of the pot.

The stain seems to prevent formation of the white crusts that so often mar the looks of clay pots. The stain also gives a deeper, richer color.

Clean the pot surfaces first. When dry, apply the stain evenly with a rag.

Sure keeps windowsills looking pretty.

Cleaning a planter

Before reusing a planter, wash the pot thoroughly inside and out with hot soapy water.

Then soak the planter for five minutes in a solution of three-quarters cup of liquid chlorine bleach to a gallon of warm water. Rinse well.

The chlorine solution disinfects the container and prevents transfer of mold or disease from the previous plant.

Inexpensive planter

From B.R.S.— I needed a large planter. But when I priced a few pots my budget said "ouch!"

Then I priced small plastic wastebaskets. Under $2. Perfect!

I could select from a variety of colors, styles and sizes. The one I chose looks pretty, and the plant it holds is thriving. A real bargain.

Bottle cap cover

To keep soil in a planter from seeping out yet let the water drain adequately, you need to partially block the drainage hole.

A bottle cap right side up makes a perfect cap for a drainage hole. The serrated edge will let out water but practically no soil.

So much handier than a broken piece of crockery.

Foam "pot shards"

Plastic foam packing "peanuts" make an excellent substitute for crockery shards to cover drainage holes in planters.

Tie up the plastic bits in a piece of old stocking or onion bag mesh to keep the soil from sifting down through them.

Great for making hanging planters a little lighter!

Repotting a big one

From A.H.— We wanted to repot a large plant, but I knew that if we tried to pull it up or dig it out we would break or cut the roots.

So I tipped the pot on its side (outside of course) and took a water hose and flushed the dirt right out of the pot.

There wasn't a single broken root—plus the roots all got a good watering at the same time.

The plant is now in its new pot and healthier than it's ever been.

Smoothing the way

African violet leaves are so fragile, they can wither and die just from brushing against the rim of a rough clay pot.

To protect the leaves, you can coat the rims of terra-cotta pots with paraffin.

Heat some paraffin in a pie plate or any vessel wide enough to accept the opening of the clay pot. Then invert the pot and dip the rim in the hot wax. When the paraffin hardens the pot has a nice smooth edge.

Remember always to be extremely careful when handling hot paraffin.

Mugs for greenery

From M.D.— I love coffee mugs and often buy them. However, when one gets a chip or slight crack in it, I don't throw it away. Instead I use it as a planter.

I have acquired the loveliest assortment of pots for small plants!

Plastic planters

The new two-liter soft-drink bottles make great planters and vases.

The dark plastic "seats" of the bottles can be pulled off (they are glued on) and used as shallow pots. They even come with ready-made "drainage" holes.

Add a few holes near the rims and use them as hanging planters.

Cut off the bottles themselves at the shoulder, or at any height you like, and use them as vases for rooting clippings or as deep planters.

They're attractive, and they're free!

CARING FOR PLANTS

Moist environment

If you have to leave your plants unattended during short out-of-town trips, try this:

Water all the plants the day before you are to leave. On departure day, place each plant in a plastic bag large enough to completely cover pot and foliage. Secure the bag at the top.

In the case of large plants too heavy to lift, slip the plastic bag over the plant and tape the bag closed to the pot.

Hanging plants, too, can be encased in a plastic bag. Secure the bag at the top with a twistie.

The effect of the plastic is that of a terrarium, preventing moisture from escaping the environment, yet leaving plenty of room for the plants to thrive and grow.

Automatic watering

From M.R.— Vacations always bring the problem of how to water the plants while you are away.

I solved the problem by putting my plants in the bathtub. I submerged ordinary bricks in water in the tub and then placed the clay pots atop the bricks.

The porous bricks and clay pots absorb enough water to keep the plants moist for many days.

A towel under the bricks will protect the tub.

Foil that feline!

From D.D.— Here's an idea to prevent your cat or kitten from digging up your potted plants.

Our cat faithfully practiced that ritual every day

until I came up with a perfect and decorative solution.

I placed some well-shaped pine cones in the tops of the pots, completely covering the soil.

I can water the plants right through the pine cones but the cat apparently doesn't want to scratch its precious paws on the prickly cones.

I hope this works for others who have pet and plants in conflict.

Keeping things straight

I'm a houseplant nut and have scads of them. To keep track, I write down on a label the kind of plant, its watering care, fertilizer needs, and any other pertinent information. Then I tape the label to the side of the pot.

When we are on vacation and have someone taking care of the plants, the "plant sitter" has all the necessary information, and I don't have to worry about my "pets."

Also, when entertaining, I find that guests notice the info. It's a great conversation starter.

How to dust leaves

A hint for indoor gardeners: When you are ready to dust leaves, slip on a pair of soft cloth work gloves. Put one hand under a leaf and gently dust with the other.

Terrific, too, for brushing cobwebs off outdoor plants in summertime.

Tending cloth gardens

To dust fabric flowers, just use your hair blow dryer on "cold."

Works beautifully.

Treat plants right

From E.K.— There always seems to be more light coming from one side of the room or the other in my house. This tends to make my potted house plants grow in a lopsided fashion.

I get around it by turning the plants periodically.

After all, plants are entitled to "equal opportunity," too.

Flood control

Here's a tip for lovers of African violets. To avoid getting water on the leaves, insert a small funnel into the soil and pour the water through it.

The leaves will be untouched and no water will spill onto the table or whatever surface the pot rests on.

Try the funnel method on other small plants, too. Especially those that fill the pot almost to the rim.

Watering aid

Here's a suggestion for watering small plants.

Use an empty plastic squeeze-type container partly filled with water.

Since the water comes out in a small stream, there is little chance of overflowing or drowning the plant.

To clip sprigs

As plant lovers know, you have to clip the tiny new sprigs on such plants as coleus and Swedish ivy to keep the plant bushy and full.

But because they are so tiny, it's hard to clip the new sprigs with your fingertips without damaging the other leaves.

So use cuticle scissors instead of your fingers. The scissors do a good job and make the chore much easier.

Egg-shell diet

Egg shells contain valuable nutrients for your plants.

Save egg shells, soak them for a day or so in a lidded container of water, then treat your plants to this fertilizing drink. They will flourish.

Fishy story

Do you have a small fish bowl or aquarium requiring you to change the water two or three times a month?

Don't throw away the water taken from those containers.

Just use that water on your house plants. No more buying high-priced fertilizer or plant food.

Your plants will grow like wildfire!

Fish diet

From M.M.L.— When I thaw frozen fish, I use the water on my house plants.

Great fertilizer.

More plant hygiene

A mild solution of water and liquid detergent will kill many kinds of insects on houseplants.

Just spray the leaves with the solution, especially the underparts where bugs usually hide. It may take several applications to do the job.

Plant pins

When potting small plants and vines, especially orchids, you need to anchor each young plant in the potting mixture.

Old-fashioned three-inch hairpins do the trick beautifully.

Recycled floor mats

When replacing the old floor mats in your car with new ones, don't throw the old ones out.

They make excellent knee pads when you are weeding your garden or flower beds.

Tracking lost tools

Searching for mislaid gardening tools is such a nuisance. Why not buy a jar of fluorescent paint at the hardware store and paint all the tool handles?

That makes the tools easily seen and quickly retrieved!

Rust enemy

Try using a pail of clean dry sand mixed with a little oil as a storage place for small garden tools. The sand will retard rusting.

Ouchless job

Here's what to do with sticky, thorny branches when you trim a rose bush.

On the ground, stretch out a length of string long enough to tie up the branches. On top of the string put down several layers of newspaper.

As you trim, stack the branches on the newspaper. When the job is done, roll the newspaper around the branches and tie with the string.

You can carry the bundle to the trash heap without ever coming in contact with the thorns.

Rose bush hygiene

From P.G.— You'd be surprised what three table-spoons of ammonia added to a quart of water will do for your roses.

With 23 rose bushes to care for, I was spending a fortune on commercial insecticides.

Then I came up with the idea of spraying the ammonia solution under the leaves and elsewhere on the bushes to rid them of bugs.

My roses are fresh and healthy. Even spiders curl up and die, and there's no harm done to the roses.

Color code

From D.R.A.— Here's how I identify my day lilies for transplanting.

While the lilies are in bloom, I tag the stems with the colorful little twisties that come on bread wrappers. I use yellow, orange and red twisties to identify lilies of the corresponding colors.

Months later when all the bulbs look alike, I can lay out the plants in any color scheme I want by consulting the tags.

Bracing large plants.

Use nylon net to tie up large blooming yard plants that have a tendency to fall over while in bloom or during rain or wind storms.

Nylon net is practically invisible and can be used over and over again.

SEED TIPS

For even seeding

When planting grass seed by hand, try mixing the seed with a little white flour.

That makes it easy to see where you've sown the seed and thus you can spread it more evenly.

Of course, the flour won't hurt the seeds or soil.

Avoiding mold

When you collect and dry seeds for use the next year, try placing the seeds on blotters.

The seeds dry faster on the absorbent material and mold is less likely to form.

Easy seed collecting

When gathering seeds from your flowers to plant the next year, here's how to save time—and your back as well!

Just pull the plants over an upside-down open umbrella and shake vigorously.

So simple, as all the seeds drop into the umbrella.

Going to seed?

Here's another easy way to collect flower seeds from your choice blooms.

Simply slip an old nylon stocking over the bloom and tie it shut around the stalk.

After the bloom goes to seed, it can dry out naturally inside the stocking, and the seeds will drop into it.

Seed identification

Save your plastic foam cups and meat trays to make

never-fading and never-rotting flower and vegetable seed markers.

Simply cut strips from the foam cups or trays and mark in waterproof ink the names of the seed varieties. Stand each foam marker in the soil beside the seeds.

Bur remover

To get those pesky burs and seeds off your clothes after a walk in the woods and fields, just rub them with a wad of cotton.

Usually they will stick to the cotton.

Socks and other knit materials need to be stretched a little while you rub. If the seeds still cling to the knit, then slide your thumbnail along behind and slightly under the cotton, thereby lifting the edges of the seeds.

Good riddance!

HANDLING CUT FLOWERS

Safe transport

From H.A.— Carrying cut flowers in the car can be quite messy.

I've discovered that it can be done without their turning over at quick stops or sharp turns.

Take three one-pound coffee cans, clothespin them together at the tops so they form a cloverleaf pattern, and I guarantee they will not tip over.

Watering arrangements

When you receive a beautiful flower arrangement

from the florist, sometimes the water in the bowl or vase needs to be changed. The sad part is that after changing the water, you can't seem to get the flowers back as they were.

So—if you don't want to disturb that beautiful arrangement, use your oven baster (that thing with a small nozzle on one end and a rubber bulb on the other). With it you can remove all the stale water and replace it with fresh water, without disturbing so much as a petal.

Well worth the effort. The flowers stay as pretty as the day they arrived.

Carrying cut flowers

When taking cut flowers to friends, dampen the stems and wrap them in paper towels, then in aluminum foil.

The foil will keep in the moisture and will cling to the stems without being fastened with a rubber band or string, doing away with the possibility of cutting off circulation in the stems.

Flower fact

If you put a few drops of liquid bleach in a vase full of water, it will stay rancid-free until the flowers are ready to be replaced.

Foam flower arranger

Plastic foam meat trays make great flower arrangers. Cut a section of foam to fit the bowl or vase you wish to use, then punch holes in the foam with a nut pick and slip the flower stems into the holes.

Floating petals

Press a small nail or tack in the cut end of a rose. The blossom will float beautifully in your rose bowl.

CARING FOR PETS

Pets and Pills

From S.R.— Ever had to give your dog a pill or capsule two or three times a day? Easier said than done . . . until I remembered how my little dog loves cheese.

When I have to give my dog a pill, I first give her one or two small tastes of cheese. The third morsel has the pill pushed into it. If the cheese is at room temperature, you can easily push the pill into it.

I have found that most dogs like cheese, so it's good to give it as a treat once in a while.

Hot-weather "heart"

During hot summer weather it is best to leave dogs at home, rather than in the car while you are shopping.

A parked car becomes an oven within minutes, even with the windows opened a few inches. For example, if it is 85 degrees outside, the inside of your car will reach 102 in 10 minutes. In 30 minutes, the temperature inside the car can get as high as 120.

Just think how hot it would get if you left your pet while you shopped around for even an hour! No one wants to return to their car to find their pet has suffered terribly, or perhaps even died.

So, please, remember how much better off they

would be left at home with plenty of cool, clean water.

Pets on the go

From E.K. — Traveling or visiting with a dog in tow can be upsetting to the pet because of the strange surroundings.

My little dog refused to eat when visiting my daughter out of state, though we had visited her many times before.

After a couple of days of the dog refusing to eat, I began to get concerned. Then I thought to set her food and water in the car. She promptly and happily gobbled it up in the familiar surroundings, and my problem was solved.

Hope this helps other travelers who take their pets along.

Diapers no, dogfood yes

Do you have a problem with field mice or other rodents chewing into your dog's large bag of food kept in the garage?

You would think you could buy a plastic pail or can with a lid to hold the dog food. But the ones with lids are usually much too large and those of the appropriate size don't even have lids.

The thing to do is to invest in an old-fashioned diaper pail. It has a lid, is large enough to hold all the dogfood, and is cheaper than most other containers.

The lid fits snugly so the food stays fresh and, best of all, no bugs, moisture or mice can enter.

Another advantage is that one does not have to struggle with a large bag to lift and pour—just scoop out what is needed, replace the lid and that's that!

Luscious leftovers

From T.S.— I have one big dog, one small dog and a cat. I buy the largest, cheapest bags of dog food and dry cat food, and save all my bacon drippings, used vegetable oil and soups.

I mix two or three tablespoons of those tasty leavings with water and pour the "cocktail" over the dog and cat food.

My pets love it. It keeps them healthy and their coats shiny.

Keeping pads soft

As a dog ages, he may develop hardened, cracked pads—especially if he runs frequently over concrete sidewalks, parking lots, roadways, etc.

A cure is to rub creamy hand lotion into his paws before he runs.

In fact, if you cream each paw in turn every day just before running time, all his pads will be puppy soft.

For cat fanciers

Cats are adorable but, oh boy, how they love to scratch! Entice that little feline away from the furniture by constructing his own scratching post.

An old log nailed to a sturdy base makes a dandy post, but could get messy. Better is to take a board and attach carpeting all around it. Again, nail it to a sturdy base—and rub a little catnip on it to really catch Tabby's interest!

As for the plants, wrap some lengths of nylon net around the base of the plant, covering the soil. You can still water through the netting, but usually it will discourage a cat's advances.

If your pet really is adventuresome and refuses to

obey the house rules, load a water pistol with water and keep it ready. It may be the solution. Just a little squirt in your cat's face (cats hate water) when he misbehaves can give him the idea in one shot! No harm done—just a lesson well learned.

Afterward, give that little bundle of fur a hug and I hope he or she keeps out of trouble.

Painless discipline

From S.D. (age 9)— I have four cats. When they don't behave I squirt them with water from a plant mister.

The water doesn't hurt them, and they have quickly learned that the squirt means punishment for doing something bad.

Tender loving care

Those of you who knit or do crafts involving the use of yarn should save the scraps.

Snip them into short lengths for easy handling by the birds, then put them outside on a windowsill, bush or tree—anywhere the birds can see them.

They will whisk the yarn scraps away to line their nests, softening the interiors for newly hatched baby birds.

SEWING SAVVY

Bobbin trick (1)

It is so exasperating when you are sewing and the bobbin thread runs out—especially if you don't have a reserve bobbin to match the thread you are using.

But you don't have to unthread your needle to reload the bobbin.

Just pull enough thread through the needle to start the bobbin, then place the bobbin on the bobbin-winding shaft. Now fill the bobbin as you would normally do.

When the bobbin is filled with thread, remove it, tighten the wheel, and you are ready to sew again.

Take care, however, both before and after filling the bobbin, to adjust the thread tension on your machine so the thread does not break.

Bobbin trick (2)

From E.A.— I used to get so discouraged when the bobbin thread ran out in the middle of a sewing project.

So now when I fill a bobbin, I color a few feet of thread toward the beginning with tailor's chalk. When the chalked thread shows up during sewing, I know I am reaching the end of the bobbin.

Bobbin switch

If you run out of spool thread while you're sewing but you have an additional bobbin with matching thread, don't despair.

Just slip the bobbin over the thread spool post and proceed as if the bobbin were a spool.

So simple.

Bobbin holder

Here's how to make yourself an inexpensive and practical bobbin holder.

For the base of the holder use a piece of rigid plastic foam (such as appliances and other fragile items are packed in these days).

Place slender nails or long heavyweight pins into the foam at desired intervals. Then drop the bobbins

over the nails, and wind the end threads around the
tops of the pins to prevent tangling.

The foam tray stays neat, the bobbins are easy to
get at, and you can always tell at a glance what you
have.

Don't lose your bobbins

Here's a terrific way to keep bobbin and matching
spool of thread together when not in the machine.

Put a piece of double-sided sticky tape on the top
of each spool and press the bobbin on it. Then stack
the double-decker item in your thread tray.

When you need to thread the machine, matching
colors are neatly filed together. There's no rummaging in two places to find the right thread and then the
matching bobbin.

One piece of sticky tape will last for many stick-
ings and unstickings.

Sort your spools

If you do a lot of sewing but don't have space for a
tray large enough to hold all your thread spools,
store them in plastic bags.

Just sort the spools by color—all the reds and
pinks in one bag, say; all the oranges and rusts in
another—whatever is handy for you—and keep the
like spools in clear plastic bags tied with a twistie.

When you need a particular color, just reach for
the appropriate bag.

You'll save time when searching for a particular
shade, and the bags can be dropped in any drawer
for easy storage.

Keep that needle threaded

Here's a way to stop your sewing machine needle

from coming unthreaded each time you complete a piece of work.

Place a scrap of cloth beside your machine for sewing onto when you reach the end of a seam. Backstitch if necessary, then proceed ahead onto the scrap of cloth and leave the needle in it.

Then cut the threads loose behind the scrap, freeing the completed seam, and move on to the next seam. When your needle has moved into the new seam, cut the scrap loose.

Keep the scrap handy and your machine will never come unthreaded in the midde of a job.

Fast thread change

For a fast spool change on your sewing machine when you want to change a color or type of thread, break the thread close to the spool already on the machine, then tie on the new color with a square knot and change spools.

Gently pull the thread through all the tension stations and through the eye of your needle, and you're ready to continue sewing.

All tied up

Before you put your sewing machine away, tie the bobbin and top threads together.

When you reopen the machine, the needle will not have come unthreaded.

Pin magnet

From F.S.— I attached two strips of self-sticking magnetic tape to the front of the head of my sewing machine.

Now I can just "toss" straight pins in the direction of the tape and they stick! So handy when sewing a heavily pinned item.

You must use steel pins, of course.

Red alert

Paint the flat side of sewing machine needles with red fingernail polish.

When it's time to replace a needle, you can easily spot the flat side for fast insertion.

Needle saver

To prevent your sewing machine needle from snapping when you stitch heavy materials such as denim, rub the fabric with a bar of soap along the line of stitching.

If you are sewing overlapped seams and some of the soap is visible after you are finished, simply iron over the soap with a medium hot iron and a scrap of clean cloth. The cloth will pick up the soap residue.

Thread saver (1)

Here's some sewing sense. When you are dropping a hem, save the thread removed from the garment.

If it's all crinkly and zigzaggy, just pull it under a warm iron—the way you would a ribbon—and it will straighten out.

Then thread it on an empty spool. When you are ready to sew the new hem, the matching thread is at hand.

Thread saver (2)

From D.A.L.— When shortening a garment, I save the removed thread on a plastic tab or twistie.

I wind the thread around the tab or twistie wire and then secure it to the garment by attaching it to a buttonhole or belt loop.

I often have to lay a garment aside in the middle of an alteration, but this way I never lose the matching thread.

Found patches

No need to spend money for iron-on patches to repair worn spots and tears in clothing.

Use scraps of fusible interfacing or scraps of appropriate weight cloth on the inside.

They do the job just as well—and they're free.

Recycled pattern paper

Scraps of pattern paper left after you cut out a pattern come in handy when machine sewing terry cloth and pile fabrics. When sewing, use the paper over and under such materials.

No more catching all those tiny loops on the pressure foot or the teeth of the feed dog.

Starch for single knits

From D.C.P.— I used to dread sewing single knits for T-tops and T-shirts because of the way the material curls to the wrong side.

Well, I've found help.

A little spray starch applied to all cut edges makes single knits easier to work with, but doesn't make them too stiff to sew. The starch can be washed out later.

Stitching guide

Machine-sewing and need a stitching guide? Try a narrow strip of medium-weight sandpaper placed face down on the fabric.

It won't slip out of place and the line of stitching will be straight and true.

But be sure to stitch along the edge, not on the sandpaper itself.

Tip for nylon

When machine sewing nylon, always place a piece of paper underneath the cloth. That way the cloth won't slip.

When you are finished sewing, just tear the paper away.

Point turner

Keep an orange stick (used to care for your fingernails) near your sewing machine.

It's perfect for turning points on collars, belts, and so on, and there's little danger of poking a hole in the material.

Easy rip

If you have trouble picking up the thread when ripping a seam, try using a fine crochet hook.

Works like a dream.

Clean machine

You'd be surprised how layers of lint and fuzz can accumulate out of sight and build up between working parts of your sewing machine.

So give the machine a dusting from time to time. The crevice tool of your vacuum cleaner does a great job of sucking out all that hidden fuzz.

But be sure to remove bobbin, face plate and thread spool before vacuuming.

Use a pipe cleaner to clean the bobbin area of your machine between vacuumings.

Vinyl table protector

A vinyl rug runner makes an excellent pad to protect the surface on which you lay out a pattern for cutting.

Scissors slip easily across the smooth vinyl.

Keep those vibes down

A carpet sample makes a good base for a portable sewing machine. The carpet pile absorbs vibration, keeps the machine from moving around—and makes the neatest pin cushion.

Nimble thimble

If you have trouble keeping a thimble on your finger, try one of these tips.

Line the thimble with a small piece of adhesive tape. It will tighten the thimble ever so slightly and make it less slippery.

Or you might paste a corn plaster over the base of the nail of the finger that holds the thimble. When you are finished sewing, remove the plaster. If any adhesive clings to the skin, take it off with a little rubbing alcohol and soapy water.

Or you could dispense with the thimble altogether. Simply shield your finger with a cut-to-fit circle of moleskin. No more pricked fingers.

Safety first

From B.K.— I like to use a single-edge razor blade for various sewing jobs—ripping seams, removing buttons from old garments, cutting buttonholes, etc.—but was always afraid to keep one in my sewing basket.

Then I found that a small metal aspirin box was the

perfect size for storing a blade. The box is easy to tuck into a corner of the basket and when I reach in, there's no danger of cutting myself.

Flossy idea

If buttons seem always to be popping off jackets and jeans, try sewing them on with dental floss.

Floss is really tough and will stand up a lot longer than general-purpose 50-gauge thread.

Button saver

Before wearing a new garment, touch the threads in the center of each button with transparent fingernail polish.   The polish will seal the threads and the buttons will stay on longer.

Back saver (1)

If handsewing or other needlework seems to put a strain on your back, place a thick pillow or sofa cushion on your lap.

You won't have to bend over so far to work, and the material will be at a more comfortable height.

Back saver (2)

If you are bothered by low back pain when you sew, try elevating the pedal on your sewing machine by placing it on a small sturdy box.

Cover the box with a scrap of fabric so the pedal doesn't slide around.

See if that doesn't make sewing more pleasurable.

For pedal pushers

From M.G. — I discovered that the foot pedal of my automatic portable sewing machine is easier to control when the pedal is turned upside down on the floor.

A piece of nonskid material under the pedal is helpful, but the upside-down pedal works fine on a bare floor, too.

Fabric softener interfacings

Another use for used fabric softener sheets: they make wonderfully strong interfacings in cuffs, pockets, flaps, etc.

It's best to get the kind that are sold in solid sheets, without slits. The sheets can be pieced by placing them end to end on the machine and zigzagging as necessary.

Curls more than hair!

Keep your curling iron handy when you sew.

It's great for pressing ribbons and dress shashes by slowly drawing them through the iron. Terrific, too, for pressing zigzaggy thread removed from a hem.

You can even iron some seams with a curling iron. And you don't have to bother setting up your iron and ironing board.

Watch those curves!

From L.C. — I discovered that a wig form covered with a terry towel makes a great substitute for a tailor's ham when you are sewing a curved seam and need to press it.

No flyaway foam

Here's a solution to the problem of handling "flyaway" shredded foam rubber when stuffing pillows you have made yourself.

Just take a sheet of fabric softener—the kind with several slits in it—and put your fingers through the slits. (Use your right hand if you are right-handed, etc.) Pull the sheet up between your fingers, then wrap the solid sections over your wrist and secure with a rubber band.

You can do a whole project without fighting static electricity. Really tames that pesky stuff.

CROCHETING

Twistie crochet marker

Here's still another use for those bread twisties.

When crocheting, they come in handy to indicate your place. You can move one along at each place you increase, decrease or change a stitch.

A great way to mark your work. Sure saves ripping out mistakes.

A purl of a tip

From I.J.R.— I used to have trouble when knitting or crocheting staying with the right row all the way across the instruction sheet.

Now I just underline each row in the pattern with a different color felt-tipped pen.

It's a lot easier to stay on row 1 when it's underlined in red, row 3 in green, row 5 in purple, etc.

Easy to see

When crocheting with a light-colored thread, wear dark-colored clothing or place a piece of dark material across your lap.

When crocheting with dark thread, do just the opposite.

That way your work always stands out from the background. Saves your eyes!

Crochet case

A kid's pencil case makes a great holder for your crocheting supplies. It's just the right size for hooks, stitch marker, scissors, etc. And you can slip it right in the bag with whatever you're working on.

Needle cases

Don't throw away the plastic container that a toothbrush comes in. Use it to hold your crochet needles.

Just as good for holding needles are the glass and plastic tubes that cigars are packed in.

Place marker

Here's a convenient way to mark your place and keep your crocheting from unraveling when you put your work down.

Just secure the crochet hook, the thread and the piece you're working on with a snap-type clothespin. When you're ready to take up your work again, unsnap the pin and continue.

Straw trick

To keep your crochet thread from tangling as you work, slip a plastic soda straw over the thread or yarn.

EMBROIDERY

Home-made hoop

A large round margarine tub easily converts into a spare embroidery hoop.

Cut the center out of the lid, leaving the rim intact. Then cut the bottom off the tub, leaving its rim intact.

Snap the two rims together again, and presto! a sturdy plastic hoop.

Knot stopper

To keep embroidery floss from knotting, try running paraffin or a fabric softener sheet over the thread before you start work.

Floss guard

Here's another trick with embroidery floss. To keep a length of floss from tangling, wrap the floss around a sponge hair curler, then snap the curler shut.

As you need more thread, just open the curler and let the floss out.

Chapter 6

ON THE ROAD—AND OFF

Whether brand new or showing its age, your car is a treasure—or should be. It faithfully, uncomplainingly (for the most part!) carries you and yours on long trips and short, for business and pleasure, in every kind of weather. All it asks in return is—no, not hugs—just some tender loving care. Without that Old Faithful may become Old Nuisance.

Heavy maintenance (brakes, engine, etc.) is usually best left to the pros. But as the tips in this chapter show, there are all kinds of little tasks and touches you can handle.

These lighter jobs keep the car looking better, add to your comfort, make travel safer and easier. Best of all, doing them is fun!

—Hugs to you, HELOISE

Corrosion antidote (1)

This is a well-tested way to rid battery terminals of corrosion. Use a tablespoon or two of baking soda in a glass of water. Drench the terminals and clamps, wait a few seconds, then dry.

That should do it, but if the terminals are very corroded, carefully remove the remaining corrosion with sandpaper or a stiff brush.

After terminals and clamps are clean, cover them with a thin coat of petroleum jelly. The jelly will retard corrosion for some time.

Corrosion antidote (2)

Something new. You don't need expensive sprays or anything else to clean corrosion from the terminals of your car battery.

Just pour a little cola on the terminal posts, being careful not to spill it elsewhere.

Now stand back and watch the cola eat away all the gook and corrosion right before your eyes!

You don't believe it? You will after you try it.

Treating bumper rust

Car bumpers have a way of becoming pitted and rusty as time goes on. And no matter what kind of wax you use, you find the rust spots won't come off.

Take heart. All you have to do is wad up a piece of

aluminum foil and rub the offending spots briskly. The foil seems to scrub away rust.

But it does not actually fill the pits, which probably penetrate right down to the steel. You can cure that by rubbing the pits with a wax candle or crayon (gray is the best color) and then using the foil.

Next time it rains or you hose down the car, the wax will help prevent rusting in and around the pitted spots.

Magnet protects lock

From J.C.— After the lock on my car door froze, I started placing a magnet memo holder over the keyhole.

My magnet is in the form of a small white daisy and adds a cheerful touch on a cold winter's day.

When I unlock the door, I just stick the daisy to any metal surface inside, and it's ready to grab when I get out.

Protects against dirt, moisture that can freeze the lock or cause rust, snow and sleet, etc. So far, no more trouble getting the door unlocked.

Freshening car air

If your car's air system (hot or cold) seems to have "bad breath" when you first turn it on, tape a half sheet of fabric softener over the front of one of the vents.

Make sure that the sheet is not so large that it cuts off the circulation of the air, of course. Keep other vents open.

A fabric softener sheet under the front seat will keep the interior of your car smelling sweet at all times.

Dandy deodorant

To squelch cigarette odors in car ashtrays, layer the bottom of the tray with dry baking soda.

The powder smothers cigarette butts so that they don't burn on and on, and it freshens the air as well.

Disposable ashtray

You know how fast the ashtrays in a car can get full during a long trip. If you will keep an empty soft drink can in your car caddy, you can snuff out each cigarette in the ashtray then just drop the butt into the can.

When the can gets full, toss it into a trash receptacle and replace it with another empty can.

This way only ashes accumulate in the tray. Probably you won't have to empty it until you get home.

If convenient, you can pour a little sand in each soft drink can to snuff out any cigarettes that may be dropped in before being completely snuffed out.

Emergency traction

If your car gets stuck on ice or in snow, shove the rubber floor mats from the car under the tires, step on the gas slowly, and you'll pull away.

Using the car's mats is much easier than trying to carry around special equipment, and the mats are always available.

Battery safeguard

Confess. Are you one of those people who occasionally forgets to turn off the headlights after parking? No doubt you've had the experience of returning to the car and finding the battery too run down to start the engine.

This usually occurs in well-lighted areas or around

twilight time, because then the headlight beams are less noticeable and don't remind you to turn them off. So here's a suggestion.

Clip a spring-type clothespin to the turn signal. Upon switching on the lights, clip it to your car key chain.

When you park and take the keys out of the ignition, there is the clothespin to remind you to kill the lights—instead of killing the battery.

For the absent-minded

Now that so many motorists are "self-servicing" their cars at gasoline stations, frequently someone drives off without replacing the tank cap.

Why not attach a label to the cap with clear tape giving your name, address and telephone number?

If you should forget the cap and drive home without realizing it, hopefully your friendly station operator will give you a ring.

A second suggestion is that before you pump your gasoline, you set down the cap on the driver's seat. You can't drive off sitting on a gas cap!

Still another idea—if your front-door handle is of the right type, rest the cap on it or dangle it from the handle.

When you open the door to get back in, there's the cap!

CLEANING UP, WASHING DOWN

Car-wash tip

When you wash your car, especially if it's a new one, try using old pantyhose or polyester dishwashing pads. They do a really good job and don't scratch the finish.

Washing spoke wheels

From S.B.— Our car has spoke wheels, and my husband was having trouble getting them clean when washing the car. I suggested using foamy-type bathtub cleaner on them.

It worked beautifully!

Just spray on the foam, let it stay for a couple of minutes, then hose it off. No muss or fuss and no scrubbing, just clean shiny wheels.

Soda for bugs

Does your car get crusted with sticky bugs in summer?

Use a little baking soda on a damp cloth or a scrap of nylon stocking to remove those critters.

Rx for wax film

That so-called hot wax treatment commonly given cars at the automatic carwash tends to leave stubborn film on the car glass.

To easily remove the film, saturate a cloth with vinegar. Give windshield and windows a quick swipe.

All clear—till the next time.

Showroom finish

From C.S.— We have a new car with a metallic finish. When we washed it, the finish would always look hazy and unrinsed.

I experimented and finally solved the problem. To a gallon of water I now add a half cup of vinegar, wipe down the car with the mixture, and dry with a clean soft cloth.

Wow—a showroom finish every time!

Speedy wash

From J.W.K.— For years I've used one of those
glass-jar hose attachments to spray my yard with
insecticides and weed-killers.

I decided it might work for washing my car. After
cleaning the jar out, I filled the jar with liquid
detergent and sprayed the car. Next I attached the
regular hose nozzle and gave the car a good
rinse.

All in all, the job took less than ten minutes. And
sure enough, the car looked cleaner than if I had run
it through an auto wash.

Unusual car brush

From M.B.— My favorite car care hint is simply to
keep a new toilet-bowl brush under the front seat.

It's excellent for brushing out dirt and dust—and
for retrieving coins and other small objects that find
their way beneath the seat.

Clearing away frost

From J.S.— My husband works in a service station
and finds that many of his customers don't have an
ice scraper or have misplaced it. So he passes on this
tip:

In a pinch, rub the windshield with the back of a
plastic comb. It does a good job of removing light
frost.

Tar cleaner

From L.E.— When we purchased our new car, my
hubby said it was mine, and so it is, even to washing
it!

The other day, while soaping it down, I noticed a
lot of road tar along one side.

Since I didn't have any commercial remover, I grabbed a can of pre-wash stain spray and sprayed away.

I finished washing the rest of the car and when I came back to that side, lo and behold, all the tar just wiped right off.

Thought some of the guys might like to know this too.

Inside tip

Try cream kitchen wax to clean the interior of your car. It removes all the road dust, shines the chrome and polishes the leather dash too.

COMFORT AND CONVENIENCE

Back exit

Do you find getting out of the back seat of a two-door car rather precarious?

If so, next time get up and, facing away from the door, step out backwards.

It's a lot easier on the knees, and you don't risk falling on your face.

Arm cooler

Even in these days of air-conditioned cars, you can still get "driver's arm" when the sun beams in through the window. On a blistering day, you drive in discomfort.

So improvise a loose-fitting sleeve out of any remnant of cool cotton material and carry it in the glove compartment.

When the sun shines in on your side, slip the sleeve over your arm. Pin it to the shoulder of your blouse or shirt and drive in cool comfort.

Not so hot

When you decide to go shopping on a hot day, take along a bath towel to drape over the steering wheel to keep it cool while you are in the stores.

When you return to the car, place the towel on the car seat and sit on it.

Then the car seat won't burn *your* seat!

Keeping cool

Does your car have bucket seats, or other seats with tilting backs? If so, on hot, sunny days lean the seat as far forward as it will go.

When you return to the car, you'll find the seat nice and cool instead of cooked by the sunbeams.

Gear-shift mitt

From C.K.W.— While on a visit to the Southwest, I noticed my hostess having trouble grasping a hot gearshift lever after her car had been parked a while in the sun.

Well, here's the perfect solution—and a great gift for folks in such warm climates. It's an insulated oven mitt.

These mitts come in colorful patterns and look quite snappy when slipped over the gear-shift knob.

And they stay cool enough to grip no matter how hot the sun.

For faster service

Tape your auto license-plate number on all your gasoline company credit cards.

When you pass the card to an attendant, he has the plate number right in his hand. Makes things easier and quicker for both of you.

Speeds up registration at campgrounds, too.

Emergency measure

When your automobile club membership card arrives, do this.

Immediately write down the phone number of your nearest tow service on the back of the card and tape a dime to it.

Might come in handy.

Car finder

Slip a red or green plastic tube (used to protect golf clubs) over the aerial of your car. The brightly colored tube makes it much easier to locate the car in a big parking lot.

The tubes cost less than a dollar, so if one is stolen, no great loss.

They do not interfere with radio reception.

Write it down

From G.W.— Do you often wonder how many miles you have driven in a year or how much gas mileage you are getting?

I stick a piece of adhesive tape to the dashboard and write on it, in ink, the mileage at the beginning of the year or the start of a trip.

That way I always have handy the basic figure from which to calculate my correct mileage driven and gas consumption.

A handy holder

You know how hard it is to find pen and paper while

driving, or a place for the turnpike ticket, or a spot for directions where you can get at them easily.

The cure is to slip two large elastic or rubber bands over the visor, spacing them a few inches apart.

Makes a convenient holder for pens, papers and other items you want close at hand. Just park them under the elastic bands.

Swatter suggestion

Always carry a short-handled fly swatter in the car.

Then when the inevitable pesky fly or mosquito gets inside the car, you're prepared.

Trash bags—gratis!

Have you ever wondered what to do with those plastic bags you find hanging on your front-door knob with samples of merchandise or advertisements from stores?

Well, here's the answer. Use them for traveling trash bags in your car . . . just hang on a convenient knob. They work just fine.

Parking accurately

Ever find after you've parked the car in your garage that you couldn't get out or you didn't have enough room to walk around the car?

Well, you can install a homemade gadget that will make parking in a tight space easy. All you need is a length of string and a small ball—a tennis ball or pink rubber ball works fine.

Here's what to do. Position your car properly in the garage, leaving the necessary room to get out and maneuver around it.

Wrap one end of the string around the ball. Then

let out enough string so that when you attach the other end to a rafter or a hook on the ceiling the ball just touches the windshield of your car—preferably on the driver's side.

Now when you pull your car into the garage you will know precisely where to stop by the position of the ball on your windshield.

Any rubbery object can be used in place of a ball—a rubber dog bone, for example.

Key caution

This tip may well save you a lot of mental anguish and a hefty locksmith's bill.

When leaving your car, never press the lock button down on the inside (as many people do) and then shut the door.

You take the chance of forgetting your keys in the ignition.

Much better to use the keys in the lock to depress the button. You'll always know where the keys are: in your hand!

Beware loose objects

Sure, most folks are aware of this danger. But even so, it won't hurt to refresh your memory—and warn those who don't know about it.

Never, but never, place anything on your car's rear window shelf.

In case of a collision or a sudden stop to avoid one, momentum could cause the article to become a flying nuisance. Hurtling forward, it could cause severe injury to occupants of the car.

TIPS FOR TRIPS

How to be sure

Did you ever leave the house to go on a trip and later couldn't remember if you turned off the stove, the iron, the water or whatever?

Well, when you turn off any of these things, say out loud to yourself, "OFF OFF OFF" as many times as you think necessary.

Then later when you ask yourself—or someone else asks you, "Oh, did you remember to turn off such and such?" you'll recall saying OFF OFF OFF. So you can answer "yes" with confidence.

No more leaky bottles

From J.K.— Many of my weekends are spent following ice hockey. Traveling means carrying liquids in my suitcase.

This may seem obvious, but before packing plastic bottles containing shampoo, lotion or the like, I open each one, squeeze it and continue squeezing while I replace the cap. This creates a vacuum, so air is constantly trying to get into the bottles, rather than liquid out.

What an easy way to avoid seeps and messiness!

Avoiding spills

Do you travel with perfume, shampoo or other fluids in your bag, like J.K.? Here's another way to seal bottles that works on glass as well as plastic.

Carry a small candle among your toiletries. Before leaving on a trip and when packing up to return, use the candle to seal the bottles.

Just light the candle and drip wax around the stoppers and caps.

Wax works better than adhesive tape to prevent leakage. Just make sure to hold the bottle and candle over an ashtray so the hot wax doesn't drip on furniture or carpeting.

Pack in plastic

When traveling, pack each garment in your suitcase in a separate, clear plastic bag. You can easily see what is where, and you will easily be able to slide out any garment without disturbing the other things in your suitcase.

The air retained in the bags helps to prevent wrinkling, too. Serves as sort of an air cushion.

Save large plastic produce bags from the supermarket and use them for sweaters, shirts and underclothes. Use large bags from the drycleaner for slacks, jeans and other large items.

Overnight bag

From B.J.C.— When traveling by car, instead of taking each piece of luggage into the motel every night, I place just enough clothing for two days' travel in a small bag, plus nightclothes and cosmetics.

It's certainly a pleasure not having to drag all of the bags in each night.

Night light

From A.G.— When we travel and plan to stay in motels, my husband takes along a little night light in his shaving kit.

We plug the light into the bathroom shaving socket. The soft glow keeps us from bumping into things if we have to move about a strange room at night.

Pillow Ploy

From S.S.— Pillowcases are so useful while traveling. Whenever we go on a long car trip, I take a pillow with three or four pillowcases, one atop the other, on it.

When the top pillowcase gets dirty, I just strip it off and there is a clean one all ready underneath.

We use the dirty cases for laundry and toys.

Survival kit

From B.M.— My husband and I travel quite a bit and do enjoy a cup of coffee as soon as we get up.

I took an old makeup suitcase and made what we refer to as our "survival kit."

It contains a two-cup coffee pot, two mugs, spoons, coffee, powdered creamer, sugar, sweetener, etc. Now we can enjoy that first cup upon awakening.

The case also contains hot cocoa, tea bags, instant grits, instant soup, a jar of processed cheese and individually packaged crackers.

Any time we want a little snack, it's available.

Bright light

From H.C.A.— I like to read before going to sleep, but find when I travel that many motels do not use light bulbs bright enough to read by. So I always bring a reading bulb with me.

Soon as we settle into a motel for the night I put my bright 100-watt bulb in the bedside lamp, if necessary.

In the morning, before we decamp, I replace it with the motel's bulb.

I'm always ready for the next dim-light stop.

Avoiding excess baggage

When you return home from a vacation trip, make a list of all the clothing and other items that you actually used—and note, too, those that just took up space.

Slip the list in a pocket of your suitcase. Then consult it when getting ready for your next trip. You'll avoid being weighed down with a lot of unnecessary baggage.

Postcard special

From L.T.— When I'm about to go on an extended vacation, I address a sheaf of peel-and-stick labels to all the friends and family members I know I'll want to write to.

I never have to ask myself in the middle of the trip who I've written to. My labels—or their absence—tell me.

Hanging loop

From J.R.— Know that loop in the back of men's coats and jackets? I have learned that it's helpful while traveling to slip this loop over the hook of a hanger before putting the coat on the hanger in the usual way.

The coat won't slide around and it won't fall off the hanger.

Emergency I.D. (1)

From G.M.— Here's a hint for travelers.

Keep on your person your motel key or a pack of matches from the motel, plus an address and phone number where authorities can reach your family in the event of an emergency.

Many times, husband or wife individually leave the place they are staying temporarily for a shopping tour or a gas fill-up. The only address they carry with them in case of accident, or whatever, is the one for back home which is miles and miles away perhaps.

Consequently, the spouse cannot be reached quickly and might be left at the motel for hours wondering what happened.

Emergency I.D. (2)

From A.D.— When we start on a trip, I print on a card our names, whom to contact in case of emergency (at home and at our destination), the name of our hospitalization insurance company, and the number of our policy. I tape this card to the dashboard in the most conspicuous place I can find.

I keep a card of this kind with all information, including the name of our family doctor, blood types, etc., taped to the dashboard even for around-town jaunts.

Heaven forbid an accident, but in case of one, I'd like anyone investigating it to have all the information they need to help me and my family.

CAMPING AND PICNICKING

How to handle charcoal

So many people complain that a large sack of charcoal takes a lot of the joy out of a camping trip. The bulky sack is sure to spill soot and mess up fingers.

Next time, before starting out, try measuring into

strong paper grocery bags the quantities of charcoal that will be needed. Staple the bag tops to prevent spilling.

The bags will stack nicely in the car, and when you are ready to cook you need only to place a bag on the grill. You don't even have to handle the coals, getting black soot all over your hands and clothing.

Useful also are cardboard egg cartons. Briquettes fit snugly into the carton just like eggs. The cartons stack neatly and when you burn one on the grill, it ignites the charcoal.

Buckle it open

Just when you reach that nice picnic spot, you realize you forgot to take along a bottle opener. And all the drinks are the kind that come in bottles with lift-off type caps.

Don't panic. Your seat-belt buckle will pry those caps right off. Try it!

The brighter the better

It seems to be a law of camping that whenever you need the can opener it's at the bottom of some box of supplies (which box?) or lost somewhere in the car or the tent.

So take along a brightly colored length of ribbon or yarn and tie the opener to an appointed spot in the car or tent.

Now you'll know where to find the darn thing.

Making a camper bed

This hint is for us poor souls who have trouble making the bed that juts out over the cab in a camper.

Before starting the trip, spread out sheets, blankets and bedspread on your bed at home just as they would go on the camper bed. Then fold over each end of the heap twice.

At your campsite, just drop the bedclothes package on the camper bed and unfold.

Not making a camper bed

Since camper beds over the cab are so hard to make up, maybe us poor souls should just not bother. Here's a clever way to duck the job.

Take two sleeping bags (the kind that open out flat) and zip them together to form one full-sized bag. Lay it on the camper bed.

Unzip the outside edge, climb in, zip up. Next morning, unzip again, climb out. Then presto! You (or whoever is last to leave the bed) zips up once more and plumps up the pillows for a nice neat effect.

Soap foils soot

You can take along even your best pots when you go camping, provided you take care when cooking over an open campfire.

The trick is to coat the bottom and sides of the pot with soap.

Then the soap, not the pot, gets black from soot and smoke. You can quickly and easily wash the soap right off—leaving the pot gleaming, and you with more time for fun things.

Sweeter to sniff

From J.M.— I like camping but hate the sour odor of dirty clothes after a trip.

I find that if I have each person in the family keep fabric softener sheets in his bag of soiled clothing, both inner and outer garments smell a lot fresher.

Makes laundering them so much more pleasant.

Caution with cutlery

If you carry plastic wrap or aluminum foil with you on a picnic, slip your sharp knives inside the roll, then replace the roll in its box.

You won't forget where the knives are, and there's no chance of accidentally stabbing a finger.

Solar water heater

To get warm water for washing up after a picnic, pour a gallon or two of water into a heavyweight black plastic trash bag. Close it with a twistie and set it in the sun for an hour or so while you're eating.

You can fill a plastic milk jug or metal bucket, enclose it in the black trash bag and get the same result.

Black plastic absorbs a lot of heat from the sun. The heat, trapped inside, warms the water. Neat!

All-purpose shampoo

A super-handy item to take on a trip is a plastic bottle of baby shampoo. It's mild, unscented and comes in an unbreakable container.

You can use it for many things!

You can shampoo (of course), shower, wash garments, wash off the windshield, wash dishes when you're on a picnic—all from one space-saving bottle that tucks easily into your shoulder tote bag.

Quickie wash up

When going on a picnic, fill an empty plastic liquid detergent bottle with water and just a few drops of detergent. Pack with a clean rag or kitchen towel.

When it's time for wash-up, just pull up on the dispenser spout and you'll have clean hands in a hurry.

Saves so many steps to a wash basin across the park.

Such a bottle is also handy to keep in the car for a quick cleanup when traveling. Useful too for farm people who do so many jobs out in the fields.

Cleaning your tank

The water holding tank of your recreational vehicle can be cleaned while you are traveling by filling it with water and a little soap or detergent.

As you ride, the sloshing of the water will clean the tank.

Make sure to empty the tank completely and rinse it well before you refill it with fresh drinking water.

Chapter 7

PERSONAL BEST

Looking good and feeling good, that's what this chapter is all about.

And the place to check it out is somewhere you can really relax, like the bath. So before you read another word, stop right here, go turn on the tap and draw yourself a delicious soak.

Throw in some lemon slices or some oatmeal (see later in the chapter)—don't forget a foam pillow— then slide in and savor all the hints for taking good care of yourself. You deserve them!

(But please don't drop the book in the water.)
—*Enjoy!* HELOISE

LITTLE LUXURIES

Cozy comfort

From C.E.W.— I never found a robe or bed jacket very satisfactory for reading in bed. The first was too bulky. The other didn't keep me warm where I was cold—across the chest.

I solved the problem with an old cashmere sweater. I keep it folded on the shelf of my bedside table and slip it on backwards when I want to read.

The sleeves don't slip and the "front" doesn't open.

I'm always warm and I don't have to get up to put it on or take it off.

Such a pleasure!

Book prop

Here's another hint for those who love to read in bed.

Lay a pillow or a facial tissue box on your stomach, then put the book you are reading on top of it.

Takes all the strain off your arms and shoulders.

Works in an armchair, too.

Mop massage

A small sponge dish mop is the handiest thing for applying a deep-heating rub to sore muscles of the back and shoulders.

Squeeze a dollop of the salve onto the sponge and rub away.

Keep the sponge in a plastic bag secured with a twistie and use it only for rubs.

It's a great help for folks with arthritis in reaching those otherwise hard-to-get-at places.

Tennis ball massage

When no one is around to rub away that pain between your shoulders, place a tennis ball between your back and the wall.

Move this way and that to massage where it hurts.

Sure feels good!

Itch extinguisher

Did you know that nylon net makes a wonderful back scratcher?

Cut a strip 18 inches by 27 inches, sew curtain rings on the ends for handles, slip it over a shoulder and scratch away.

Divine!

Back rest

A thick piece of foam rubber makes an excellent back rest in the bathtub so one does not have to lean against a cold tub.

No need to buy an expensive bath pillow. Just squeeze the water out of the foam after your bath.

Easy tub exit

This is for those who find it difficult to get out of the tub after a bath.

First, empty the tub. Then turn over to a kneeling position, push up to a standing position, and make your exit.

Use a damp washcloth on the edge of the tub to keep wet hands from slipping.

Lemon refresher

From C.K.— The one time of the day when I really pamper myself is during my evening soak in the tub. In hot weather, I've found that sliced fresh lemons floating in my bath water really help take off oil and perspiration after a hot, busy day.

I cut slices of lemon and drop them in the tub while running hot water. The heat helps to release the juice in them and their natural astringent action is gentle enough for my usually dry skin.

Another bonus of a lemon bath is the room-freshening power of even one or two lemons. My bathroom smells great, as does my skin, the towel and even the wastebasket after I have discarded the slices.

Oatmeal bath

Here's a tonic for dry skin—a luxurious soak in an oatmeal bath.

Cut out two five-inch squares of cheesecloth or cut off the feet of an old pair of nylons. Put a quarter of a cup of old-fashioned oatmeal (the slow-cooking kind) into each square or stocking foot and tie up with a twistie.

Run a shallow tubful of very hot water and drop the oatmeal bags in. Let them sit for 15 or 20 minutes.

When ready to take your bath, add the rest of the water and adjust to a comfortable temperature.

When you emerge, you will find your skin feeling nice and soft without that tight, dried-out sensation.

Kitchen steambath

Save energy, money and get a facial all at once by cutting short the drying cycle of your dishwasher.

Open your dishwasher right after the last rinse and before the drying cycle starts. A big cloud of steam will escape—but watch out—it's hot.

It's great for your sinuses, your skin—and in winter, the humidity is even good for your home.

Your dishes can air dry.

PERSONAL STUFF

Shower caddy

From A.L.— In my shower I hung one of those three-tier wire baskets sold in kitchen-gadget shops. In the basket I keep shampoos, conditioner, bath oil, extra soap bars, fresh washcloths, etc.

Everything needed for the bath is within arm's reach. Eliminates having to step out of the shower to get some item you forgot.

Clutter cure (1)

A beaded hanging planter makes an attractive holder for toiletries in the bathroom.

Suspend one from the ceiling over your toilet tank or beside the sink and use it for combs, brush, toothpaste and all those other things that tend to clutter the sinktop.

Clutter cure (2)

To keep your dresser top free of cologne and nail polish bottles (and who knows what else?), convert an old spice rack into a toiletries holder.

You can't have too many of these handy little racks. Keep your eye open for them at garage sales and flea markets.

Good to the last drop

Sometimes spray and pump bottles of toiletries (and cleaning products, too) don't have tubes long enough to draw up the contents at the bottom of the bottle.

The remedy is to lengthen the tube. Take the cap and plunger assembly off and simply slide a flexible plastic straw (cut to fit) over the existing tubing. Make sure the flexible elbow of the straw is near the bottom.

Make a bend at the elbow and reinsert the tubing so the straw bends to one side at the bottom of the bottle.

Now to spray up or pump up the remains of the lotion, liquid or what-have-you, simply tilt the bottle so the remaining contents flow toward the mouth of the straw.

Thrifty fragrance

Don't throw away the container after a stick cologne or deodorant is all used up.

Pop the empty bottle (with lid off) in a dresser drawer, or on the linen shelf or inside a suitcase.

The fragrance lasts and lasts. And there's no need to buy sprays or sachets.

Lingering scent

Oily skin holds perfume scent longer than dry skin. So, if your skin is dry, before applying perfume, rub a very thin layer of petroleum jelly or hand lotion on your skin.

For long-lasting effects, apply inside your elbows and behind your knees.

You will smell delicious for hours.

Perfume dispenser

Purse-sized perfumes and toilet waters are often so much more expensive than dressing-table sizes. So why not make your own purse container?

Wash out and convert an old eye-drop bottle or a sample perfume bottle. Use a dropper to transfer the scent or make a funnel out of the top of another small plastic bottle cut in half.

Jar trick

This is for women who like to keep their fingernails long but hate dipping them into jars of cream and makeup—only to come out with more cream under the nails than on the fingers.

When jars are fresh, use a tiny spoon (such as those some ice cream stores give with a sample flavor) to scoop out what you need.

Once you have made a dent in the contents, simply turn the jar on its side. You'll be able to finger out a dollop of cream without getting it under your nails.

To keep jars on their sides from rolling around on your cabinet shelf, lay them on a strip of thin foam rubber cut to fit the shelf.

Blush stretcher

When there's not enough powdered blusher left in a compact to fill a brush, grind the leftover contents into a powder with a spoon and add a few drops of moisturizer to the powder.

Presto! Cream blush.

Thick and thin

A few drops of witch hazel added to the bottle will nicely thin liquid foundation that has thickened.

But you might want to leave the makeup unthinned in the bottle. Simply wet your face first and the foundation will slide on smoothly.

Also, slightly thickened foundation is great to use as concealer under the eyes and over blemishes. Then there's no need to buy a special product for cover-ups.

Facial flannel

If you are fed up with the high price of facial tissues and "cotton" balls (today they seem to be made of rayon or polyester), make your own reusable make-up-remover cloths from old flannel pajamas, baby receiving blankets, etc.

So soft, and washable, too.

Baby your eyes!

From M.D.V.— This is for women who wear mascara—and have to deal with the problem of getting it OFF!

Oils and cleanser make my eyes burn, soap dries my face, and special eye makeup removers invariably irritate my eyes.

I was really at a loss until I discovered those oil-treated baby towelettes. They are gentle to the skin, yet half a sheet takes the makeup off both eyes. So economical.

Do-it-yourself pads

You can make your own pads for removing eye makeup or fingernail polish.

For makeup removal, pour some baby oil into a clean jar, then add cotton balls. Put the top on the jar and let stand. The cotton balls will absorb the oil. Or fill the jar with cotton balls first and dribble a few tablespoons of oil over them.

For your manicure kit, add a little nail polish remover to a jar of cotton balls.

Saves having to moisten a cotton ball each time you need one.

Take care, however, not to confuse the two jars should you prepare both kinds of removers. You don't want fingernail polish remover anywhere near your eyes!

Outsmarting smudges

From T.M.— I always used to apply eye makeup after I had put on my foundation and blusher. But I recently learned a better way.

Apply eye makeup *before* foundation. That way when you steady your hand against your cheek—as you stroke on eye shadow, for example—you will not smudge your face makeup. No face makeup yet to smudge.

Since you don't have to worry about smudging, you'll be more relaxed and do a much nicer job on your eyes.

Carrying case

A plastic toothbrush holder makes a neat and nifty container for carrying makeup brushes, eyebrow pencils and such in your handbag.

No more caking

To keep a compact of pressed powder from caking, always store the puff upside down in the case. It's the oils from your skin that make the powder cake.

Roller switch

From J.W.— Need a makeup sponge in a hurry? Wash out the foam roller of a hair curler and use that.

Also, you don't have to buy special packaged-for-makeup sponges. Polyurethane (not cellulose) sponges sold for kitchen and general use can be cut to size to suit your makeup needs. They come in pretty colors, too.

Pencil logic

If you use those nice pencil and crayon-type eye-shadows and lipsticks, you know how difficult it can be to sharpen them. Sometimes you lose almost an inch of pencil because the innards just crumble away.

Trick is to put your pencils in the fridge overnight, or even in the freezer, when you see they need sharpening. A chilled pencil sharpens like a dream. And you hardly lose a bit.

For better blending

Here's another terrific eye-makeup tip. After you apply eye-pencil color, gently smudge and blend it using the cap of the pencil.

You don't waste a cotton swab. Your fingers don't get messy. And since the cap doesn't absorb the color, you don't waste any of the pencil either.

GOOD GROOMING

Showering efficiency

Next time you take a shower and wash your hair,

shampoo and rinse your hair first thing, then put on conditioner.

By the time you have washed the rest of you, the conditioner has done its job and is ready to be rinsed off.

No more standing in the shower waiting for the conditioner to work.

Saves on hot water, too.

Brush first

Brush your hair before you wash it. You won't have a drain full of hair.

Keep wet to set

If it becomes inconvenient to put up your hair right after you've washed it, just pop a shower cap on to keep your hair damp until you are ready to set it or rewet with a plant mister.

Dye protection

Rub a layer of petroleum jelly around your hairline and over your ears before coloring your hair. The excess will wipe right off with no scrubbing necessary and without leaving telltale dark smudges.

Dye stain remover

If you forget to rub your brow with petroleum jelly or some dye reaches an utreated part of your face or neck, you can remove the stain with toothpaste, of all things.

Just rub it over the tinted area, wait a few seconds and the stain will be gone. That's all there is to it.

Berry stain cleaner

To remove berry and other fruit stains from your

fingers and the skin around your nails use a little denture cleaner.

Just a bit on a nailbrush whisks those stains away.

Foil cap

When you are giving yourself a home permanent and you are ready to cover your hair, do it with a sheet of aluminum foil.

The foil will stay in place over your curlers without being tied or pinned.

Ear cap

Are you always getting sticky ears from hair spray?

Well, cover each ear with the cap of the hair spray when you spray that side.

It's a lot easier to wash the cap than your ears!

Electric roller cleaning

Yes, you can wash the rollers of an electric hairsetter. (But you can't wash the heating unit!) Here's how:

Scrub the rollers with a brush in soapy water, then rinse. Be sure to let them dry thoroughly before replacing them in the unit.

If the unit gets soiled, unplug and rub the dirty area with a dampened cotton swab. Just don't let any moisture near the heating elements.

Incidentally, if your heater no longer heats, you can put those curlers in a pan of boiling water to heat them. Retrieve them from the water with tongs.

Foam bath

From M.K. — While cleaning the bathroom sink I accidentally sprayed foam bathroom cleaner on my comb and brush (also awaiting cleaning).

In seconds both were shining!

Now I no longer soak comb and brush in ammonia —just spray with foam, run comb through brush a few times, rinse thoroughly, and that's it. What a time-saver!

Roller bath

To clean your foam or plastic hair rollers, drop them in a bag of nylon net or a plastic mesh bag such as onions come in and toss them into the washing machine.

Curler-pin keeper

To end the clutter of electric hair curler pins, buy a four-slot adhesive-backed toothbrush holder.

Organize your pins by size and slip them into the slots. So much easier than having to rummage through a bag of pins.

You can fasten the holder to the wall of your bathroom or inside a cabinet if you prefer to keep the pins out of sight.

Loop a roller

From T.H.— I've contrived a curler that's really comfortable to sleep on.

I bought a batch of those soft sponge hair rollers and removed the plastic rods and clasps.

To replace the plastic clasps, I cut half-inch wide strips across the legs of a pair of old nylon hose.

Using a bobby pin, I thread a stocking strip through the hole in each roller. This leaves me with a loop extending out each end of the curler.

Now I roll up my hair on the sponge curlers, then slip the loops over opposite ends. They stay securely in place. And they couldn't be less bothersome. No rods poking into your scalp!

The first time you try this method, you may find undoing the curlers a bit tedious. If you hurry you may not get each loop unfastened. But with a little practice, you'll have no trouble.

For tender scalps

From M.L.— Since I have long hair and a tender scalp I find most hair rollers are too heavy for me. Instead I use empty toilet paper rolls.

The cardboard absorbs some of the moisture, and my hair seems to dry faster than it does with conventional uncomfortable rollers.

If you want rollers with a diameter smaller than the paper rolls, simply slit the core down the middle and overlap the cylinder until you reach the desired size, then tape in place.

End-paper substitute

If you like to set your hair in brush rollers, try using squares of nylon net instead of paper end-papers.

The nylon net tucks in hair ends easily and the little securing picks go right through the netting.

And of course you can reuse the squares indefinitely.

Brush replacement

When the bristles on brush rollers wear down, do this:

Take a larger sized brush out of its roller and put it inside a smaller roller.

The added bristle length will hold your hair securely. And you'll have to replace only the largest sized rollers.

No tangles, no frizz

If you run out of hair conditioner, you can use fabric softener instead (but only on undyed or nonpermed hair). Dilute a teaspoonful in a glass (preferably plastic) of water and pour over your hair.

Or use a fabric softener sheet. Simply rub it over your damp hair. Then rinse.

Rub your comb and brush with the softener sheet, too.

No more static-y hair!

For fluff

On the other hand, if you are troubled by limp hair, even though you "just shampooed the day before," try eliminating all fabric softeners and conditioners.

Fabric softener in towels and pillowcases is easily transferred to your hair.

You'll be fluffier without them!

End static cling

In winter when you are wearing knit dresses, slips and tights, you can beat static cling by simply rubbing the legs of your tights or the skirt of your slip with a used fabric softener sheet. Or, for that matter, ever so slightly, with a fresh sheet.

Slick trick for men

Some men swear by this recipe for an easier shave, said to leave the skin smooth as a baby's.

Rub a little baby oil on your face before applying shaving cream. The razor will just glide through your whiskers.

A particular boon to those with sensitive skins— or who simply dislike shaving.

Warm it in water

You menfolk out there—put your can or tube of shaving cream in the hot water in the bathroom sink when you wash hands and face.

When you are finished washing, the shaving cream will be just the right temperature for shaving.

No need to buy so-called hot-lather machines.

Soft landings (1)

So many people break dentures by having them fall into the basin while cleaning them.

A good solution is to line your sink with a washcloth. Then if you drop the dentures they make a safe landing instead of shattering.

It helps, too, to fill the basin part way with water. The water will break the fall rather than the teeth.

Soft landings (2)

Want to be more stylish about it? Try keeping a square of plastic foam—the color of your bathroom decor, no less!—rolled up in a pretty napkin ring in your medicine cabinet or on your dressing table.

When your dentures need a wash, just spread out the foam sheet on the bottom of the basin. The foam will cushion an accidental fall.

The main thing is to protect those dentures somehow. Because sooner or later—you're bound to drop them!

Contact lens bath

A small glass spice jar with a perforated inner lid makes an excellent container for washing contact lenses.

You can wash your lenses, drain the wash water,

then rinse, without risking losing a lens in the sink.

Keep the jar handy in your medicine cabinet.

Emery board extender

An emery board all worn around the edges is often still good in the middle.

So just slice an old board down the center with scissors, and you'll get two more long sides for filing your nails.

Sharpens your scissors, too!

Cuticle care

If you are troubled by tight cuticles that cling to the base of the nail, try to give yourself a manicure frequently to keep those cuticles from getting out of hand!

Soak your fingertips for five minutes in warm water and vinegar (equal parts). Then apply glycerin or a glycerin-based lotion, massage and gently push cuticle back with an orangewood stick.

Rx SENSE

Medication color code

Here's a helpful hint for those with weak eyesight.

If you have a lot of medicines, code each bottle with a piece of adhesive tape that you have colored with a crayon or marker.

Then on a sheet of paper make a guide to the bottles. Color squares to match each bottle and beside each square indicate the name of the medicine, when you have to take it, and how much. Then post the sheet inside your medicine cabinet door.

Much easier than having to read the small print on those little bottles.

Top tip

If you forgot to ask the pharmacist for an easy-open cap on a plastic vial of medication, don't despair. You can easily convert a child-proof cap to an easy-open cap.

In the case of a two-part safety cap, simply discard the inner disk and use the other part to seal the vial.

Another sort of child-proof cap has a tiny plastic nib inside the rim of the cap. It is easily shaved off with a small paring knife.

Of course, if there are small children in your home, be sure to store easily opened vials out of their reach.

Medicine to go

When traveling at home or abroad, always carry all prescription drugs in their original containers.

If you are going to be away for any length of time it's wise, too, to carry a copy of each prescription. Saves trouble if you run out—and with customs officers.

Help in a hurry

From L.B.— I'm a heart patient but have other medication to take as well as heart pills.

To make for quick identification, I have painted a red heart in fingernail polish on the lid of the heart medication.

Now if I need that medication in a hurry or someone else needs to get it for me, there'll be no mistak-
ing which bottle contains the proper medication.

Of course, one should still check the bottle label.

Dosage control

Do you have to take a medication before bedtime?

When you complete the evening meal, set out the
exact dose in a separate bottle.

No more wondering later whether you actually
took the medication or just thought about it. A
glance at your after-dinner vial will tell you.

Besides, although it's important that you take a
medication, it's just as important not to take it twice.

Securing a bandage

Ever have trouble getting an adhesive bandage to
stay put over the cut tip of a finger?

Here's the remedy. Make a lenghtwise cut down
the center of each adhesive end-strip, cutting only as
far as the pad. Remove the paper backing and cover
the cut as usual. Then cross the half-strips at each
end so the bandage is secured by an "X."

Works handily!

WARDROBE HINTS

New and blue

If you like your jeans looking new and blue—and
want to help keep them that way, here's what to do.

Turn them inside out before washing and drying
to prevent streaking.

Wash in warm water and don't hang in direct
sunlight.

Every five or six wearings treat them to a dry cleaning.

Military crease

From C.L.— Do you hate to iron jeans? I do! But my husband likes his jeans ironed with a crease.

He taught me a trick he learned in the Navy.

When he buys new jeans, I iron the crease in, using plenty of spray starch, before I wash them that first time.

Would you believe, the crease stays in wash after wash? Just a light touch-up with the iron and the jeans look as though you've spent lots of time on them.

A great time-saver and a happy man!

Spot concealer

If your jeans mysteriously acquire bleach spots ("But they were nowhere near the bleach!"), you can repair their appearance with a blue crayon.

Rub over the spots until they are covered, feathering the color outward to blend inconspicuously with the denim. Then place wax paper over the spots and press with a hot iron.

Repeat as necessary. The jeans won't be good as new, but they'll pass muster.

Keeping a secret

If you don't care to advertise the size of your jeans but don't want to remove the leather tag at the waist, you can just erase the size with a regular pencil eraser and a little elbow grease.

So easy.

Convertible jeans

From C.E.P.— Sometimes I wear my favorite blue jeans with low heels and sometimes with high heels.

With the low-heeled shoes I fold under the legs and "hem" them with masking tape on the inside.

When I change to high heels, I just remove the tape.

Hose saver (1)

Tired of ripping your pantyhose when you zip up your boots?

Place a sheet of paper between your leg and the boot and pull both paper and zipper along together. Smooth!

Hose saver (2)

Don't you just hate it when you poke the nail of a big toe through sandalfoot pantyhose or stockings?

Try spraying the toes, and heels as well, with hair spray. You will get many more wearings out of your hose. Hair spray stops runs, too.

Another way to protect nude hose is to cover the edge of your big toenail with transparent first-aid tape.

Belt preserver

To keep a fabric belt from wrinkling and looking worn long before the dress it matches does—stiffen it with iron-on mending tape. The tape will give the belt enough body for many more wearings.

Belt hangers

Save those tabs that come on soft drink cans and hang them over the necks of dress hangers so you can keep dress and matching belt together.

Bend the tab up—then hang the belt buckle over the tab.

No more lost belts. And no more belts cluttering the closet floor.

"Sweet rolls"

If you buy scented toilet tissue, don't throw the paper tubes away. Use them as sachets in drawers and closets.

Sure makes sense to keep scents to save cents!

Hose keepers

Toilet tissue tubes are ideal for storing pantyhose and stockings. Write on the outside of the tube what's inside and its color and condition—for example, "black sheers, run in thigh").

The tubes stack neatly in your drawer, and there's no rummaging through a tangle of hose to find what you need.

Sweater saver

When a favorite sweater begins to grow thin at the elbows, don't abandon it.

Cut a patch from an old nylon stocking and sew it to the inside of the sleeve in the elbow area.

The patch will not show and will keep the sweater wearable for many more seasons.

Non-slip shoulders

If you like to wear a shoulder bag but find it difficult to keep one on your shoulder, glue a strip of felt to the inside of the strap.

Your bag will not slip.

Snap it up!

Who hasn't struggled trying to catch that hook or loop above the zipper in the neck of a dress that zips up the back?

Well, instead of a hook and eye (or thread loop), sew in a snap.

Sew the flat piece of the snap on the left side. Then take the other half of the snap and sew it on (through two holes only) as close to the edge on the right side as you can, so the snap projects beyond the edge of the cloth.

Now you have only to press the two halves of the snap together.

No more exasperating episodes trying to hook yourself together.

Bracelet trick

Here's the solution to another exasperating problem: how to fasten a bracelet clasp when you really need two hands to do the job.

And it's so easy. Just tape one end of the bracelet to your wrist. Then it's a cinch to bring the other end around and slip the prong into the ring.

INDEX